The Secret of Laughter

The Secret of Laughter

Magical Tales from Classical Persia

Shusha Guppy

LONDON · NEW YORK

Published in 2005 by I.B.Tauris & Co. Ltd
6 Salem Road, London W2 4BU
175 Fifth Avenue, New York, NY 10010
www.ibtauris.com

In the United States of America and Canada distributed by Palgrave Macmillan, a division of St Martin's Press, 175 Fifth Avenue, New York, NY 10010

ISBN: 1 85043 427 1
EAN: 978 1 85043 427 6

A full CIP record for this book is available from the British Library
A full CIP record for this book is available from the Library of Congress

Library of Congress catalog card: available

Typeset in Bliss by A. & D. Worthington, Newmarket, Suffolk
Printed and bound in Great Britain by TJ International Ltd, Padstow, Cornwall

Contents

Acknowledgements

A wise and generous friend, Ted Hughes urged me to write these stories and publish them — 'they are part of the soul-heritage of Persia' — during a conversation about his rendition of Ovid's *Metamorphoses*. Joan Leigh Fermor was a wonderful source of warmth and encouragement. I am grateful to both and cherish their memories. I also wish to thank Patrick Leigh Fermor, mentor and guide, Brigitte Marger, Gerry Croghan, Dr Leonard Lewisohn and, especially, Robert Chandler, for their numerous kindnesses. Many thanks are due to Gillon Aitken for his gentle support always, and to Ayesha Karim.

For Zahra, in memoriam,

and for Isabella, Lorcan and Edmund

Foreword

Close your eyes so that sleep doesn't get into them,' said Zahra, as she gently closed my eyes and continued with the story. This was a well-known trick mothers used to make their children go to sleep, and it always worked — tired after a day of activity the child would soon fall asleep, content with the promise of another story the following night.

Zahra was a young girl who looked after me when I was a child. She came from the Northern provinces, Mazandaran, on the shores of the Caspian, and she had the guilelessness and good nature that Iranians attribute to Northerners. She became part of our household as an orphan at the age of twelve, and later when I was born, she adopted me as her pet. During the day I followed her everywhere as she went about her chores, at first tied to her back, then toddling behind her, and at night I listened enthralled to her stories, until I was lured into sleep.

In the Persia of my childhood there was always a favourite story-teller among the women of the household: a mother, an aunt, a frequent visitor or a retainer. Whatever their functions and activities during the day, at nightfall these women set them aside and turned into magicians, conjuring an enchanted world where imagination was enthroned. The tales they concocted of princes and princesses, orphans and dervishes, jinns and giants — *divs* — winged horses and flame-breathing dragons, miracle-working saints and invulnerable heroes fascinated and entertained us, nourished our minds and souls, and laid the foundation of our imaginative lives.

Some of these stories, I later learnt, came from Persian classical literature, but the majority were folk tales and fairytales that had been passed down orally, varying in details and conclusions according to the temperament and talent of the story-teller, their provenance lost in the mists of the past.

Some came from Firdowsi's epic poem *Shahnameh* — *The Book of Kings* — Persia's national epic, which the story-tellers embroidered with often-quoted lines from his poetry at moments of climax. Others were tales of dervishes and saints, from the works of Attar, Rumi and other Sufi poets and visionaries. They transmitted perennial wisdom, and moral and ethical guidance. But the folk tales and fairytales that Zahra told me I never found anywhere else. Had she invented them? Or had she picked them up as a child in her native Mazandaran? Travelling in Persia many years later once or twice I came across a *naqqal* — professional story-teller — in a *chai-khaneh* — tea house — in some remote village, whose story rang a bell.

Before the advent of radio, cinema and television, story-telling was one of the most popular forms of entertainment, and the *naqqal* a familiar figure in the country and among the tribes. He went from village to village and became a well-known figure, and a favourite in his area. As soon as he was spotted on the edge of a village, children rushed to greet him with cries of 'The *naqqal* is here!', 'The *naqqal* has arrived!' A noisy cortege of urchins and idlers followed him to the middle of the village square. To enhance his dignity and his hieratic status, he often dressed in the garb of a wandering dervish — a woollen cloak, a felt hat, a staff and with a boat-shaped begging bowl hanging on his belt. As the crowd swelled, everyone asking for his favourite story, he began by chanting a prayer and some lines of poetry in praise of God, the Prophet and Imam Ali[1] before beginning his story. A one-man show of dazzling virtuosity followed, a play with a large cast in which the *naqqal* acted all the parts, male and female, human and animal, casting a spell over his audience with the assurance of a star violinist playing a Stradivarius. He elicited exclamations, awe, imagination, approval, condemnation, hoots of laughter or tears of pity, rejoicing in his power over the audience. When the highest pitch of tension was reached and expectation became unbearable, he suddenly stopped and asked for contributions. Coins flew from all directions and landed at his feet, which he picked up with slow dignity, then continued the story to its dramatic *dénouement*, in which invariably the villain met his fate and the lovers were united at last.

To make sure that the moral of the story was not lost on his audience, the triumphant story-teller enlarged on it, telling the young to beware of the snares of Fate — Greed, Arrogance, loss of Faith — and to trust to Providence. 'The Infinitely Merciful, All Compassionate'[2] would come to the rescue. Redemption was achieved through Love, Compassion, Self-Abnegation and Magnanimity; happiness was the reward for Virtue and Patience, and there was a higher order in the universe which we who were mere mortals could not fathom but which explained our tribulations and sorrows. A few lines of memorable poetry by the wise Saadi, the lyrical Hafiz, the ecstatic Attar or the saintly Rumi would close the performance and send everyone home enlightened.

In bad weather, the *naqqal* performed in the *chai-khaneh* in the village Bazaar, often for no other gain than the pleasure of entertaining the clients and cheering their spirits. I once heard a *naqqal* in a tea house in Isfahan tell the tragic story of the great hero Rustam — the Achilles of Persian mythology — and Sohrab whom he killed in battle, only to discover too late that Sohrab was in fact his long-lost and only son.[3] There were tears in every eye in the audience as he described the fatally wounded young Sohrab dying in his father's arms, extolled his purity and courage, and conjured up Rustam, the invulnerable hero before whom the strongest warriors trembled, crumbling in lamentation; and then the final redemption as the armies of both sides laid down their arms to mourn.

Written in rhyming couplets at the end of the tenth and the beginning of the eleventh centuries by Firdowsi, Persia's Homer, the *Shahnameh* tells the history of Persia from its mythical beginning to the Arab conquest in the seventh century AD, which ushered in the Islamic era. It begins with the creation of the world and the advent of civilization — the invention of the arts, the establishment of laws and customs and institutions. The poet then chronicles the history of the nation through a chain of fifty kings and their reigns, hence the title of the book. Woven through the narrative are philosophical reflections, moral injunctions and lyrical exaltations, expressed in limpid, memorable poetry.

Many of the characters and stories of *The Book of Kings* echo those of Greco-Roman and Indian mythologies, which indicates their common Indo-European ancestry. For example Jamshid, the mythical king credited with the introduction of civilization and the invention of wine, is identified with the Indian god of the underworld, Yama, and the Greek gods Prometheus and Bacchus, while Rustam, the invulnerable warrior and hero, is similar to Achilles, and other stories bring to mind tales from the *Iliad* and the *Odyssey*.

Telling the imaginative history of ancient Persia and its people, the *Shahnameh* has become the symbol as well as the custodian of national identity through the country's long turbulent history —

wars, invasions, revolutions, periods of decline and threats of dis-integration come and go but with the *Shahnameh* the idea of Iran and the Iranian people endures.

Chanting the verses of *The Book of Kings* in the *zur-khaneh* — traditional gymnasium — to the beat of a hand-drum as the athletes perform their ancient exercises and their martial arts, and telling the stories of wise rulers and intrepid heroes in tea houses and public squares, reminds Iranians of their history and their tradi-tions. It heightens their sense of continuity and cohesion.

Similarly the stories of Rumi and Attar and other Sufi masters hand down their spiritual history of the Persians after their en-counter with Islam. They combine the wisdom of Zoroastrians with Islamic mystical doctrines and philosophy. Drawing from Hebraic religious traditions, they express an ecumenical and uni-versalist vision that through the power of poetry has been transmitted down the centuries and seems particularly appealing today, hence Rumi's present popularity in the West.

The *naqqal*'s market fluctuates according to circumstances. It seems that after the revolution of 1979, when the accent was more on religious than historical and national identity, *naqqals* almost vanished from the scene; religious ceremonies and the commemo-ration of saints and martyrs were the rule. But in recent years, in spite of competition from television, the cinema and the Internet, *naqqals* have come back.

If the public figure of the story-teller was the male *naqqal*, with his bent for epic, heroic and moral tales, at home story-telling was the prerogative of women; it was an expression of their creative and educative gifts. They had the imaginative freedom to digress, change, embroider, expand and invent their fairytales and folk tales, creating endless variations. Their objective was to entertain, thrill and enchant as well as to pass on ideas and beliefs and traditions. Disenfranchised, and denied any political or administrative role in public life, in the private sphere of the family Iranian women wielded absolute power. They managed their households, controlled their children's upbringing, and through their husbands and sons and brothers they influenced society and the course of events. The folk tales and the fairytales they told their children were part of their upbringing, and played a considerable role in forming their characters and their personalities. Thus women were not only the biological mothers of the nation, but the creators and transmitters of its cultural inheritance. This explains the recognition by modern psychology[4] 'of the important place which folk and fairy tales have acquired in the mental life of our children', as Freud states. 'A recollection of their favourite fairy tales takes the place of memories of their own childhood; they have made fairy tales into screen memories.'[5]

In the patriarchal society of Persia, where the law favoured men and discriminated against women, Persian women had to rely on their strength of character and inner resources, and they drew on a variety of stratagems to survive and exercise power. One of the most effective of these was the telling and spinning of stories, and since most of the population was unlettered, they passed them down the generations by word of mouth; they were the guardians of memory.

The archetypal example of a woman who through the magic of story-telling saves her life and changes her own destiny and the course of events is Sheherazade, the protagonist of *The Thousand and One Nights*. Apart from Zahra, and inspired by Sheherazade, the story-tellers I remember from my childhood — my aunts and a spinster cousin, who often came and stayed for long spells with us — often set their stories in Baghdad at the time of Haroon al-Rashid, while others preferred more exotic settings such as Rum (Byzantium), China and, above all, India, where some of the stories of *The Thousand and One Nights* are said to have begun.

Many years later I found echoes of these fairytales and folk tales of my childhood in Western literature — Homer, Ovid, Shakespeare and Racine. Perhaps this is because the creation of myth and the intuition of the supernatural belong to the deepest level of the human spirit and are part of the imaginative heritage of humankind. The link is deeper than the gap. For example the story of 'The Padishah and His Three Daughters' brings to mind *King Lear*, while the transmutation of the bodies in 'The Secret of Laughter' echoes Ovid's *Metamorphoses*. Except that in the Persian tales any changes are not due to the arbitrary powers of some capricious god — 'the heavenly crimes of the gods' as Ovid puts it — but to the deeds of men. They are the results of actions by sorcerers and magicians, individuals of exceptional knowledge and special skills, which they can use as they wish, for good or ill. Responsibility rests with the human being, who is sovereign and in possession of free will. The characters counter the arbitrary whims of Fate — or the tyranny of the Ruler/Magician — with ingenuity, cunning, dissimulation and on occasions a little helping hand from the supernatural.

Sometimes Providence intervenes through a prophet or an imam in a dream, and sometimes in the shape of the enigmatic figure of Khizr, who returns very rarely from the *Alam-e-Gheib* — the Occult World — where he dwells, to guide or rescue an innocent soul. Khizr, who often materializes out of the blue, is the 'servant of God' whom Moses encounters in the desert and who becomes his companion and guide. The story of their journey together is told in the Quran (Sura XVIII, 59–82), but its origin goes back much further to the epic of Gilgamesh and to Alexander's search for the Spring of Immortality, while in Jewish legends Khizr is identified with the prophet Elijah. Thus he is the symbol of the Spirit, the divinely inspired knowledge. He can be identified with the Old Man in Western fairytales who 'always appears when the

hero is in a hopeless or desperate situation from which only pro-
found reflection ... a spiritual function ... can extricate him'.[6]

Khizr can be the Poet's Daemon, often identified with the
earthly person who has inspired the poem. For Jaluddin Rumi,
Khizr is the beloved friend and spiritual master Shams-al-Din
Tabrizi, who speaks through him and is the true voice of his
ghazals — the sonnet's Persian counterpart:

Speak, sun of Truth and Faith, pride of Tabriz!
For it is your voice that is heard through my utterance.

In their Persian versions these tales of metamorphosis, of poverty and riches, blind Fate and human ingenuity emanate from the
collective psyche of a whole people. They express their longing for
a fairer dispensation, a less arbitrary rule in a dangerous and ruthless world. They reflect Persia's Zoroastrian belief in the
permanent contest between Good and Evil in the world and within
the human soul, as well as her Islamic faith in the sacred harmony
of the universe and God's justice and mercy. They soothe and
encourage and warn, and they make us believe that change is possible, that Man is free, and that in the end virtue is rewarded and
wickedness is punished. They illustrate the traditional virtues of
courage, generosity and *adab* (formal courtesy) in a society where
until recently literacy was the privilege of the few.

Above all, these stories extol and celebrate the Feminine: their
protagonists are mostly women whose patience and prudence,
beauty, love and strength save the day for their men, whether
fathers, husbands, sons, lovers or rulers. These women are the
agents of cohesion and transformation, the power behind the
throne, the counter, the curtain or the Veil.

In these stories it is often the women who initiate the love
affairs, make the first move, determine the outcome of events and
overcome the obstacles that Fate and the patriarchal society scatter

in the path of love and fulfilment. In the *Shahnameh* the mother of the great hero Rustam falls in love with his father Zal and marries him despite her father's opposition. Their union is blessed with a son who becomes the saviour of his country. In 'The Story of Bijan and Manijeh', the most famous romance in the epic and a favourite of story-tellers, it is Manijeh, the daughter of Afrasiab, King of Touran and Persia's arch enemy, who falls passionately in love with the Persian hero Bijan, and uses every ruse and potion to win his affection and keep him secretly with her. When her secret is discovered she is stripped of her royal status and expelled from the city, while she remains defiant, proudly proclaiming her freedom to love, and ensures the survival of her lover until rescue comes — naturally through Rustam, who arrives with his army and defeats Afrasiab.[7]

While 'Bijan and Manijeh' and 'Soltan Mahmood and the Band of Robbers' — from Firdowsi's *Shahnameh* and Rumi's *Masnavi* respectively and included here as the archetypal and everlasting favourites of Persian story-tellers and their listeners — are safe in the poets' books, all the other stories in this collection belong to my memory and imagination, and would disappear if unrecorded. Telling them to children and grown-ups over the years, I was encouraged by their response to write them down so that I could share them more widely, and preserve them. However humble a cherished possession may be, we wish to safeguard and share it, and in due course pass it on. Just as folk songs and folk tunes whose composers and provenance are unknown have inspired classical composers — Brahms, Bartok, Stravinsky and Dvořák among others come to mind — folk tales and fairytales are a source of inspiration. These stories belong to the rich treasury of Persian folklore and writing them down is a help to their survival. They encourage hope and optimism about the future, and strengthen faith in Providence and in human resourcefulness, rare treasures in our doubting, uncertain times.

The Persian story-teller begins 'Once upon a time', which in Persian is a rhymed couplet: *Yeki boud, yeki naboud/Gheir az khoda hichki naboud* — 'There was one and there was none/Except for God there was no one'. Another couplet marks the end: 'Our story is told and you must rest/Though the crow has not yet reached its nest.' When I tell the stories to children in English, I begin with the Persian formula: 'Yeki boud, yeki naboud', and we are off.

Deeper meaning resides in the fairy tales told to me in my childhood than in the truth that is taught by life.

Friedrich Schiller

The Padishah and His
Three Daughters

There was one and there was none/Except for God there was no one.

There was once a great king, a Padishah, who had three daughters. They were called Shahrokh (literally 'with a face as majestic as the Shah's'), Mahrokh ('as bewitching as the Moon') and Golrokh ('as ravishing as the Rose'). All three were beautiful and accomplished, having had the best tutors in the kingdom to teach them poetry and philosophy, as well as the feminine arts and the ways of the world. Naturally they had numerous suitors, but the Shah wished to marry them off to the worthiest young men, the wisest and bravest in the realm.

One day he sat on his throne, flanked on either side by his two vizirs and surrounded by his courtiers, and summoned his daughters. Presently they were ushered in, dazzling in their fineries and jewellery, and the audience gasped at their beauty and grace. 'The moon has divided into three!' they whispered, 'The nightingale would not know which rose to choose!' and other such compliments.

The Padishah turned to his eldest daughter and said, 'Tell me, Shahrokh, is it the lining that protects the coat, or the coat that protects its lining?'

'The coat protects its lining, Crowned Father,' Shahrokh replied.

'Well answered,' said the Shah. 'I see that your education has not been in vain, that you are thoughtful and discerning, and you deserve a good husband. I will give you to my Right-Hand Vizir.'

This vizir was a handsome young man who had distinguished himself in battle and was said to be wise beyond his age. Overjoyed to be chosen from among the suitors, he prostrated himself before the King, kissed his feet and thanked him for the honour.

Next the Padishah called forth his second daughter. 'Tell me, Mahrokh,' he said. 'Does the coat protect its lining or vice versa?'

'The coat protects its lining, Sire, naturally,' responded Mahrokh without hesitation.

'Well done, my dear. You are worthy of no less a good man than my Left-Hand Vizir.'

This young man was just as suitable as the first, and equally delighted to be granted his secret wish to marry Mahrokh.

Finally the King called forward Golrokh, the youngest and loveliest of his daughters and his favourite, and put the same question to her.

'I believe that the lining protects the coat,' answered Golrokh.

'Surely you don't mean that?' frowned her father. 'When it rains or snows, if there is a fight or some other accident, it is the coat that bears the brunt and gets damaged, while the lining remains protected.'

But Golrokh was adamant: 'I still think, beloved Crowned Father, that it is the lining that supports and safeguards the coat, not the other way round.'

The Shah said that Golrokh was not only ignorant but stubborn and opinionated too, that her education had been wasted, and that she did not deserve any of the young men present at Court. He ordered his servants to search the city and find the lowest, poorest, most unworthy man, and let him marry and take away his youngest daughter.

'Never let me see your face again,' he roared, and banished his most cherished daughter forever.

The Shah's men searched all the poor districts and slums of the town and beyond, and eventually in the wasteland outside the city gates they found a woman living in the ruins of a hut. She was so poor that people said 'Her mattress is the hard earth and her blanket is the distant sky', meaning that she had no possessions, not even the humblest bedding. She scraped a living by gathering thorn bushes in the wilderness and selling them as firewood to townspeople.

She had a son called Hassan, who was so lazy, pusillanimous and useless that he slept in a broken *tanour* (clay oven for baking bread) and never came out. She had tried everything — entreaties, promises, threats — to make him come out and earn a living, but nothing had worked, and eventually she had given up trying. Every day at noon she would take some bread and water to the *tanour* and call out to him, and he would stretch his hand and take the food from her.

The courtiers reported to the Shah that surely this young man was the least worthy of his subjects, and the Shah ordered that Golrokh be married to him.

'My father's wish is my command,' said Golrokh calmly, and the courtiers were astonished at the equanimity and good humour with which she accepted her fate. They felt sorry for her but there was nothing they could do. All Golrokh was allowed to take with her was a dress of rough calico and a horse's blanket, but she managed to smuggle out three gold sovereigns, hidden between her two shapely breasts. Three servants from the royal household accompanied her to the gate of the town, handed her over to the Poor Woman and left, shedding tears of pity for her plight.

As soon as the Shah's men had disappeared, Golrokh began to explore the broken-down hut which was to be her home, and finding nothing by way of bedding she spread her horse blanket next to the *tanour*, where her husband hid himself from the world, and went to sleep, for all the world as if she had never slept in a proper bed, nor had known silken sheets and feather pillows. The Poor Woman was surprised at such insouciance, but she said nothing.

In the morning Golrokh gave one of her three sovereigns to her mother-in-law and sent her to a goldsmith in the Bazaar, whom she had heard was an honest man, to change into money. In those days there were no banks, but every bazaar had traders who exchanged gold and silver for cash. With the money Golrokh bought the basic household necessities and some provisions, and she hired a couple of workmen to repair the hut so that they could have a solid roof over their heads when the rains came.

The next day she told her mother-in-law to leave her son's food outside the *tanour* and tell him to come out and fetch it himself. At first Hassan refused, protesting and howling and cursing; his mother was ready to give in, but Golrokh stopped her. After a while hunger and thirst got the better of Hassan and he lifted his body out of the *tanour*, snatched the plate and disappeared inside again. Every day Hassan's food was left further and further away from his hiding place, which forced him to come out a little more to reach it.

Meanwhile with the second and third of her sovereigns Golrokh extended and improved their dwelling: the surrounding wasteland was cleared up, a well was dug to provide water, a garden was laid with a pool in the middle, trees and orchards were planted, vegetable patches created, and a wall was built round the domain.

When the work was done and the place looked fresh and dignified, Golrokh told her mother-in-law to stop putting any food out for her son. At noon Hassan called out to his mother and demanded his lunch, but she told him that if he wanted to eat, he had to come inside the house. He refused vehemently and again yelled and swore and threatened, but not daring to disobey Golrokh, who was after all the Padishah's daughter, his mother held fast.

Hassan resisted for several hours, but eventually he felt so hungry that he gave in. Slowly he pulled himself out of the *tanour* and stepped out into a dazzling new world, his eyes blinking after the darkness of his dungeon. This was not the wasteland he knew and had fled, but a beautiful garden shaded by trees and covered with flowers, a fountain splashing cool water into a blue pool of goldfish and rose-petals, birds singing sweetly in the branches. The derelict hut was now a pretty house, gleaming white in the sun.

His legs were almost atrophied from lack of exercise, but he managed to wobble to the house. Inside, he found a ravishing young woman sitting in front of a nap spread on the carpet, covered with an array of steaming aromatic dishes. He was too ashamed to enter the room, knowing that he looked like a scarecrow, but Golrokh came forward smiling, took his hand and sat him down beside herself, as if they were old friends. She put a small helping of each appetizing dish on his plate and filled his glass with fruit sherbet, urging him to eat by putting the first spoonful in his mouth herself. While Hassan was eating, she went out of the room and with the help of her mother-in-law pulled down the *tanour*, razing it to the ground and flattening the earth until no trace of it was left.

After he had eaten and drunk his fill of the superb lunch Golrokh had prepared for him, Hassan crawled back towards his hideout, only to discover that it had gone! There was nothing he could do but to come back sheepishly to the house, where Golrokh was waiting. Deep down Hassan was glad to have an excuse to stay in the house, for having tasted the good food and seen the comfortable surroundings he did not really want to go back to his dark hole.

Golrokh, who had foreseen the outcome of her scheme, had called in two bath attendants from the local *Hammam* (public baths) and they spent hours washing and scrubbing Hassan, removing the layers of grime he had accumulated over the years of his seclusion. They cut his hair and trimmed his nails, and after he was thoroughly groomed they dressed him in the new fine clothes which Golrokh had bought for him.

The man who entered the room after his bath was not the hirsute, dirty, wild caveman Golrokh had seen a few hours before, but a handsome, elegant, gentle young man, smiling at her shyly. After they had taken some refreshment, Golrokh told him that they had no money left — all her three sovereigns had been cashed and spent — and that it was now his responsibility as the man of the household to work and earn a living for them.

'But what can I do?' Hassan replied in panic. 'I have no skills, no profession. Who would employ me?'

The only thing he could expect was to become a water-carrier in the *Hammam*, which was considered the lowliest job in the world. Even that would not be easy to get, given his reputation for laziness, but Golrokh told him not to worry. She went to see the bath manager and pleaded with him, and he agreed to give Hassan a try.

Every morning at dawn Hassan left for the *Hammam*, where he worked all day, fetching and carrying huge kettles of hot water to the clients and doing their bidding. At night he returned home and handed over his meagre wages of one *dirham* (shilling) per day to his wife.

After a while Golrokh saw that Hassan was working hard and had become very popular with the clients of the *Hammam* on account of his good manners and discretion, and she thought it was time for him to move on to a better job. One day she took him to Haji Ahmad (*Haji* is the man who has accomplished the pilgrimage to Mecca), the most reputable merchant in the Bazaar, and asked him if he needed an honest, trustworthy assistant. 'Indeed I do!' replied Haji Ahmad, who had met Hassan in the *Hammam*. 'I have noticed that Hassan is modest and cheerful and willing to work hard, which is rare these days, and I will gladly take him on.'

So it was that Hassan began a new life at the chambers of Haji Ahmad in the Bazaar, where he was both apprentice and assistant. His new boss was a good man, fair-minded and mild-mannered. He had produced six children, but they had all died in infancy and recently he had lost his wife too, so he was happy to have Hassan's company and treated him like a son.

One day he announced that the time had come for him to go abroad on business, and that he wished to take Hassan with him, if Golrokh agreed. Hassan, who was now deeply in love with his wife, had no wish to leave her and his old mother and accompany his boss, but Golrokh persuaded him to go, see the world and gain some experience.

The Haji's destination was the great bazaars of Damascus and Aleppo, where merchants from East and West met and exchanged goods. Haji Ahmad would take silks and brocades, spices and nuts, and sell them to *Farangi* dealers. (*Farangi* means 'Frank', or French, and by extension all Europeans.) In those days there were no cars, trains or aeroplanes, and people travelled by horse and camel. The journey took months, even years, and was fraught with danger. Apart from illness and natural disasters, wild animals and reptiles, floods and earthquakes, the roads were infested with bandits. You were lucky if they only took your goods. Often they cut your throat as well and left you in the desert to be eaten by jackals and vultures.

The night before his departure, Hassan was walking home feeling sad and apprehensive, wondering what Fate had in store for him and already missing his sweet Golrokh. The sun had set in the western sky leaving a crimson ribbon on the horizon and the roads were empty.

Suddenly there in the middle of the road stood a young man, as if conjured out of the air, smiling.

'Good evening,' he said to Hassan. 'Give me a *dirham* and I will teach you something that will stand you in good stead on your journey.'

Hassan gave him the coin and the Stranger said, 'Always be modest. Wherever you go, enter with your head first, not your feet.'

Hassan thanked him for his advice and moved on, but hard as he tried, he could not figure out the riddle: what did the Stranger mean? And how could one enter somewhere head first? He turned round to ask him, but the young man had vanished. So he continued on his way and was soon lost in thought.

Presently a second stranger appeared in front of him, seemingly out of nowhere and just as pleasant as the first.

'Good evening,' he said in greeting. 'Give me a *dirham* and I'll teach you something that will stand you in good stead on your journey.' Having received a coin he told Hassan, 'Whenever you strike camp for the night, sleep on the highest ground.' And he walked away.

Hassan pondered the advice for a while before returning to his musing. After a few minutes a third stranger barred his way.

'Give me a *dirham* and I'll teach you something that will stand you in good stead on your journey.' Again Hassan complied and the unknown youth said to him, 'Always be patient. Wait and ponder, count forty before you act.'

At least this was something he could fathom, he thought — it was wise not to be impulsive but ponder the matter before acting — and he looked back to thank the stranger, but he had disappeared just like the other two before him. Hassan walked on and finally reached home to the tender welcome of his Golrokh.

The next day at dawn hundreds of pilgrims and merchants assembled at the western gate of the city, their mules and camels laden with merchandise and provisions, much as today travellers gather in stations and airports. Being the oldest and grandest among them, Haji Ahmad, perched on his caparisoned camel, led the caravan as it set off, bells a-jingle, to the cry of *Allah-o-Akbar* — God is Great — and the ululation of women and children. Everyone watched the long trail recede. The sound of the bells grew faint and died, the caravan became a thin line on the horizon and finally dissolved in the haze.

The road to Damascus and Aleppo was long and dangerous, going through a desert that stretched to infinity, with nothing but rocks, thorn and sand. Now and again the caravan would halt at an oasis, where a few palm trees and willows had grown around a well, and where the travellers could bivouac, feed their animals and fill up their goatskin water containers.

One day the caravan stopped for the night in an oasis and as usual a young man was sent down the well to fetch water. But instead of the buckets coming up full, they returned empty, and the young man himself never appeared. A second youth was sent down to see what had happened to his companion, but again he failed to return and the buckets came up empty. What could possibly have happened to these young men? A third, a fourth, a fifth … up to twelve young men were sent down the well, but none returned.

At last Hassan volunteered to try, but Haji Ahmad was apprehensive — had he not promised Golrokh to take care of her husband as if he were his own son and return him to her safely? What could he tell her should anything happen to her husband? But Hassan wouldn't be deterred. As he was being lowered into the well, he suddenly remembered the words of the First Stranger: 'Go everywhere head first, not feet first.' So he asked to be lowered upside down, which seemed a very strange request, but they were desperate for water and did as he told them.

As Hassan went deeper and deeper down the well and it became darker and darker he began to panic, fearing that a dragon might be there who would gobble him up at once, as it had doubtless done the others before him. He thought of Golrokh and his heart sank, but he plucked up his courage and continued downwards.

Soon a light appeared at the bottom of the well, illuminating a stream of clear water. But before he could sigh with relief he saw a huge *div* with two straight sharp horns sprouting from his head, eyes like two burning torches and long, razor-sharp nails, sitting beside the stream. Scattered all around him were the bones of Hassan's young companions whom he had killed and eaten.

There was no retreat, and Hassan thought it was the end of him too, but the *Div* said to him, 'I am the king of the world that lies beneath this desert, you are an intruder and I am going to kill you and eat you, but first tell me: why did you come down head first?'

Hassan was petrified, knowing that he was about to be torn to pieces and gobbled up, yet he had the presence of mind to reply, 'Your Majesty, I was taught to bow my head before greatness, and as you are the greatest *Div* in the underworld, to express my respect I came down head first.'

The *Div* was surprised and impressed by Hassan's courtesy. 'Well spoken!' he said. 'I can see that you are a polite young man. The others were impertinent and had the temerity to challenge my authority, so I ate them. But I'm going to reward you by allowing you to send up as much water as you wish.' Saying this he filled Hassan's buckets from the cool, limpid stream beside him and sent them up.

Imagine the joy of the travellers above! 'We are saved!' they cried, 'God be praised!', and rushed forward to drink. In a moment the buckets were empty, and were sent down for more, and again they came up full of delicious cool water, as if filled at the very *Kowthar*.[1] They all drank their fill and watered their animals and gave thanks to Allah for His bounty.

Down in the well the *Div* clapped his hands three times and a heavy metal door appeared in the wall of the well, which he pushed open, inviting his guest to enter. Hassan stepped over the threshold and found himself in a magical garden the like of which he had never seen before, surrounding a grand palace that rivalled the Padishah's. 'This is my house,' said the *Div*, 'and you are welcome to stay with me forever.'

Not in his wildest dreams had Hassan imagined such a palace, and for a moment he was tempted to accept and to forget the worries and tribulation of life in the world, but then he remembered Golrokh.

'I thank you for your generosity,' he said to his host. 'But I have a young wife, an old mother and an employer who is like my father. I love them all and they depend on me. I cannot stay.'

The *Div* was pleased at Hassan's response. 'I only wanted to test you,' he said, 'to see whether you were dutiful and strong or selfish and weak', and he invited Hassan to share a meal with him before he left. Once again he clapped his hands three times and another *Div* appeared, carrying a huge tray the size of a banquet table, covered with a variety of gorgeous dishes.

Hassan ate and drank his fill, thanked his host for his generous hospitality and asked his permission to leave. As a parting gift the *Div* gave him three large pomegranates, saying, 'Keep these somewhere safe and don't show them to anyone. They will prove useful to you.'

Meanwhile up in the desert the travellers began to worry. 'Where is Hassan?' they asked one another, and wondered what to do. Should they send another young man to find out? As they were debating the matter Hassan emerged from the well and stepped over the edge to the cheers of his companions. He told them nothing about his encounter with the *Div* or his magic domain, only that he had found no trace of the poor young men who had disappeared, and the caravan moved on.

Half-way across the desert it met another caravan on its return journey to Persia. There was great jubilation, as many of the merchants, their retinues, cameleers and muleteers knew each other, and they were delighted to meet and exchange news of home and kin. A feast was prepared for dinner and the night was spent in conviviality. As dawn struck and the sun appeared on the far horizon, painting the sky gold and crimson, the travellers embraced each other farewell and the two caravans departed in opposite directions. You can imagine how they looked back to see the distance between them grow, the dust settle, the sounds grow faint, until there was nothing left except the silent vastness of the desert.

Just before their departure Hassan wrapped the three pomegranates the *Div* had given him in a bag, put the parcel in a box and entrusted it to a friend in the other caravan to take to his wife for safekeeping until his return.

Months passed. Hassan's caravan finally reached Damascus and put up at a *caravanserai* (inn for caravans) in the Bazaar. Haji Ahmad began trading with his colleagues from Farangistan, making Hassan privy to all his transactions and teaching him the fine points of the profession.

From Damascus they went to Aleppo, and again Haji Ahmad secured some profitable deals. Finally they were ready to set off on their journey back home.

The day before the caravan's departure, Haji Ahmad gave Hassan some money saying, 'I have made a handsome profit: take this and invest it in any merchandise you choose. We will share the proceeds if you are successful.'

Hassan went around the Bazaar and noticed that everyone was dealing in textiles and spices and gems — silks and velvets, frankincense and myrrh, turquoise and lapis-lazuli. There were large quantities of citrus fruit at very low prices, on account of it being an exceptionally good year for fruit, but no one was buying any. So he decided to acquire some. He bought a dozen weights of oranges and tangerines and lemons, and loaded them on his camels. Haji Ahmad noticed Hassan's laden animals and wondered what he had bought, but discreetly kept silent.

Once again the desert crossing took many months, during which privation and illness took their toll of the travellers. Eventually they reached the shores of the Persian Gulf and embarked on a ship to cross the water to Persia.

At the approach of home Haji Ahmad's curiosity got the better of him and he asked Hassan what he had bought. 'Citrus fruit,' he replied. His boss was flabbergasted. 'What?' he yelled. 'What use is citrus fruit? You fool! There are masses of it in Persia, and by the time we get home yours will have rotted away. You've wasted my money, and I thought I had taught you to be prudent! I was a fool to trust you!'

He was so angry that he lifted his hand to strike Hassan, but the young man caught his boss's wrist and calmed him down. 'Don't worry, Sir, I'll sell the lot before we reach the Persian shore.' Saying this, he went on deck, set up trestles, spread the fruit over them and waited for customers.

Hardly had they set sail than the weather changed, the wind rose and the storm gathered, whipping the sea into a roaring monster; gigantic waves tossed the boat like a cork and made the passengers violently sick. They could eat nothing except citrus fruit, which on account of its sharpness calmed their nausea and settled their stomachs. So they gathered around Hassan's makeshift shop and bought every single orange and tangerine and lemon he possessed, at the highest price. Soon he had none left and he had trebled his investment. He divided the profit with his boss as agreed and kept his own share, intending to start his own trading chambers in the Bazaar when they reached home.

In Persia their route went through some mountainous country, twisting around precipitous ridges and down narrow gorges — a little stumble and you would fall thousands of feet to shatter on a rock below or drown in a fast-flowing torrent. At last they reached a green valley encircled by high hills, a stream running through it. It was like the Promised Land, and they rushed down to strike camp, rest and let their animals graze on the rich grass. They pitched their tents on the river bank and drank the ice-cold sweet water, giving thanks to God for having survived the most perilous part of their journey.

As Haji Ahmad's muleteers and cameleers were about to raise their tents among the others, Hassan suddenly remembered what the Second Stranger had taught him: 'Always sleep on high ground.' He told his master that it would be better for them to

sleep higher on the slope, not at the bottom of the valley. Haji
Ahmad protested, saying that it was cold and windy up on the
mountainside and that they would be better sheltered by trees and
boulders, close to the others, but Hassan insisted, saying that he
had reconnoitred the mountainside and found a cave large enough
to accommodate not only their own party but also some of their
companions and all their animals. Reluctantly Haji Ahmad gave in.
Servants swept the cave floor clean, spread carpets and beddings,
and what with fatigue and excitement soon everyone was fast
asleep.

Around midnight clouds gathered above the valley, the stars
vanished behind a black velvet pall, thunder roared like an angry
lion, and lightning ripped the sky with jagged lines of molten copper. Presently the rain began to pelt down, and what rain! It was as
if a dam had burst and unleashed a new Deluge. As always when a
sudden downpour hits the bare, parched mountainside the water
has no time to sink and the result is flood. Soon an ocean of water
was rushing down the slopes, uprooting trees, dislodging boulders,
carrying with it everything in its path. Taken by surprise, the
travellers had no time to run away and many perished, together
with their animals and possessions, swept away by the water. Then
just as suddenly as it had started the rain stopped; the water found
its course at the bottom of the valley and swelled the stream. The
crystal trickle gliding over the pebbles before the storm became a
mighty yellow river half a mile wide, rumbling and roaring like a
belligerent dragon.

Helpless and bedraggled, the survivors began to gather together and see what they could salvage. It was a calamity from
which Hassan and his party had been saved by following the advice
of the Second Stranger — 'Always sleep on high ground.'

Haji Ahmad was astonished by the foresight of his protégé. He
began to think that Hassan had *Elm-e-Gheib* (knowledge of the

Occult World) or at least some special gift of prescience. He admired him more and more, and decided to adopt him as his only son and heir. In case other disasters were in store and he perished before reaching home, he wrote his will there and then, stating his wish that in the event of his death Hassan would inherit his business, his title of Grand Merchant and all the wealth he had amassed in the course of his long life.

The depleted caravan moved on. It was the last leg of the journey, and the travellers were impatient to reach home. One night they stopped at a *caravanserai* near the town of Kashan, a city famous as much for its deadly scorpions as for its beautiful carpets. So vicious are these insects that no antidote has ever been found for their poison and death inevitably follows their sting. They say that they are the agents of the Devil and sting only by his orders.

Anyway, that night a big black scorpion crawled into Haji Ahmad's bed and stung him. He screamed and jumped out of bed. Everybody woke up and rushed forward, and before the scorpion had time to crawl away, it was clobbered to death. As for Haji Ahmad, he was treated in the usual way — they pulled out the sting and sucked out the poison. But it was to no avail — within minutes he was dead.

As his sole heir Hassan buried him in the local cemetery beside the tomb of a holy man, with all the pomp and ceremony he deserved. In accordance with the Haji's will Hassan inherited his fortune as well as his position and titles, and became the leader of the caravan for the remainder of the journey.

Well, it was Haji Ahmad's *Qismat* (Fate, lot) to die when and where he did — his time was up. The date of your death is fixed when you are born and nothing can change it. Izrail, the Exterminating Angel, never misses an appointment. I'll tell you something about him. When God appointed him as the Angel of Death, Izrail was very distressed, saying that humankind would hate him for all the loss and sorrow he would inflict upon it. He begged the Almighty to give him a task which would bring him love and gratitude instead of hatred and malediction.

But God would not desist. 'Don't worry,' He said. 'I have thought of that. I have created all sorts of diseases and accidents to end people's lives, so that they will always blame them as the causes of death, not you.'

And so it is — a scorpion or an adder appears out of nowhere, and becomes the killer, but in reality it is the Will of God carried out by Izrail, and there is a wisdom in God's decrees which we mortals can't fathom.

Now I'm sure you want to know what was happening to Golrokh all this time her husband was abroad. Well, when she received the three pomegranates given to her husband by the *Div*, she went to hide them in a secret safe in her bedroom. But as she was putting them inside, one of them fell from her hand and burst open, and lo! instead of pomegranate seeds, quantities of precious stones spread on the floor — rubies and emeralds and sapphire, and above all a *Gohar-Shab-Cheraq*.[2] Golrokh was mesmerized. The next day she sold some of the gems and with the money bought a whole district of the town adjacent to their house. She had a beautiful palace built to rival her father the Padishah's, and filled it with the most sumptuous furniture — silk carpets, crystal chandeliers, gold tableware and every other luxury you can imagine. When her own house was completed, she proceeded to repair all the others on her estate. She built *Hammams* and mosques, *caravanserais* and hospitals; she installed vast kitchens at the gates of the city to feed poor wayfarers and wandering dervishes; and the town throve.

Not surprisingly Golrokh's fame spread until it reached the Padishah himself. 'Who is this Grand Merchant Hassan who is so rich and whose wife does such good work for the population?' he wished to know, and he asked his vizirs to enquire.

Meanwhile Hassan and his retinue reached the gates of the city. Hassan could barely recognize the place — it looked so prosperous and clean, with tree-lined avenues, new buildings, parks and running streams.

He wanted to surprise his wife, so he asked his men to wait outside the city gates and went alone in search of his home. But instead of the small building he had left behind he found a palace, with gardens and pools and fountains, surrounded by a high wall. The gate was guarded by a sentry, but Hassan discovered a small back door and entered quietly into a passage at the end of which another door opened on to a hall. He was dazzled by the luxury he found within and wondered whether he was dreaming. He heard the sound of people talking in a room and tiptoed along the corridor towards it. The door was shut but through the keyhole he saw a ravishing odalisque reclining on a golden dais — Golrokh! She seemed to him more beautiful than he remembered, but who was the handsome young man sitting beside her? They were talking and laughing, holding hands and giving each other little kisses. His heart started to pound as if it were jumping out of his chest: his beloved Golrokh had forgotten him and taken a lover!

So overcome was he by jealousy that he wanted to burst in and confront her, and kill them both on the spot. But as he was about to push the door open, he remembered what the Third Stranger had told him: 'Always be patient. Wait and ponder, count forty before you act.'

So he waited, lacerated by doubt and despair. But from what they were saying, he soon realized that the handsome youth was Golrokh's brother Shahbaz, that he had been sent by the Shah to find out about the woman whose reputation for wealth and good works had reached him, and discovered that she was his own, long-lost sister. Relieved and ashamed of having doubted his wife's virtue, Hassan knocked on the door gently and entered.

Imagine the scene that followed! Husband and wife falling into one another's arms, the joy of reunion after so long an absence, the kissing and hugging and sweet murmuring of endearments, Shahbaz's delight at meeting his gentle brother-in-law about whom he had heard so much from his sister. There was so much to tell — all the adventures and incidents they had experienced during the years of separation. It was agreed that Shahbaz would not reveal to the Shah the identity of Hassan and Golrokh, but instead ask him to condescend to their invitation and grace their humble abode with his presence for dinner at a mutually agreed date. Mind you, their home was far from humble — if anything it was even more luxurious than the Shah's — but Golrokh was a princess and knew the rules and language of the Court.

Next Golrokh told her husband to go back to his campsite outside the city gates and announce his arrival, so as to be welcomed in a manner worthy of his station as the Grand Merchant of the Bazaar. She had the city gates decorated with banners and lanterns, the entire Bazaar decked out with lights and ornaments, and a long carpet spread in front of her threshold. A cortege of notables and merchants went to Hassan's campsite to welcome him back officially and accompany him to his house, where Golrokh and her household were waiting for him.

Meanwhile Shahbaz returned to the Court and told his father about his meeting with the mysterious woman who did such good work for the community, and her husband Hassan, the Grand Merchant of the Bazaar. He transmitted their invitation to the Shah, who was delighted to accept. Accordingly a date was agreed upon and transmitted to Golrokh.

On the appointed evening Golrokh had their house and garden illuminated with hundreds of torches and candles, hired the best chefs in the kingdom to prepare a lavish meal, and called in musicians and dancers to entertain her royal guests.

When the Padishah and his suite arrived, Hassan received them with full honours. They were led to an *eyvan* (domed veranda) covered with silk carpets, where a jewel-encrusted golden dais was erected for the Shah to recline on, while his vizirs and courtiers formed a semi-circle around him — the two vizirs and their wives, Golrokh's sisters Shahrokh and Mahrokh, on either side of the monarch, the rest in rows according to rank and seniority. In those days women did not accompany their husbands on such occasions, but Hassan had expressly extended the invitation to Shahrokh and Mahrokh and insisted that they attend. So the Shah had ordered his daughters to join the party.

Refreshments were served while the musicians played delightful music and the dancers performed lovely dances. They seemed the very *houris* (nymphs) of Paradise promised to the Righteous in the Holy Book, as they fluttered around like birds in their diaphanous veils and glittering costumes. The Shah was struck by the lavishness of the reception and the opulence of the Palace, which almost surpassed his own.

Presently he asked to meet the hostess, the Grand Merchant Hassan's wife, who had organized such a sumptuous feast.

'If Your Majesty so wishes, she would be happy to come and present her respects,' said Hassan.

In fact all this time Golrokh was watching the scene from behind a curtain, her heart overflowing with love for her father, who had aged and seemed rather melancholic. At a motion from Hassan the curtain parted and Golrokh stepped in, glowing in her fineries like the Morning Star. As she walked towards the royal dais, the Shah recognized her and gasped with delight. What tears of joy! What outpouring of emotion as father and daughter fell into each other's arms! The whole audience was moved, while Golrokh's sisters rushed forward to embrace her.

'How I have missed you!' sighed the Shah. 'Not a day has passed without my thinking of you, and regretting my impetuosity. But when I sent for you, they told me that you had disappeared. I thought that you had left the kingdom.'

Golrokh laughed and kissed her father, saying, 'Didn't I tell you, Beloved Father, that the lining protects the coat not the other way round? Woman is the lining, man is the coat, and it is the woman who makes the man, not the reverse.' The Shah gladly admitted that his daughter was right, that it was woman's support and protection that ensures the happiness and success of man.

He ordered the whole town to be decorated and illuminated with myriad lights for Golrokh and Hassan's official wedding. The wedding ceremony took place at the Royal Palace, prayers were said in every mosque for the newly weds, and the celebrations continued throughout the kingdom for seven days and seven nights. Golrokh and Hassan lived happily ever after and had many children.

Now I'm sure you wonder who the Three Strangers were. They were Hassan's Luck. In life much depends on luck, but if Hassan had been foolish and not listened to the advice of the Three Strangers, he would not have survived as he did. Luck comes in many guises, but most people don't recognize it or don't take advantage of it. For Hassan it first arrived with Golrokh and he seized it, instead of being stubborn and sticking to his old lazy ways. So his luck came back when he needed it, taking the form of three young men he met on the road.

But what is luck?
You may well ask!

Our story is told and you must rest
Though the crow has not yet reached its nest.

The Thief and the Cunning Bride

There was one and there was none/Except for God there was no one.

Long, long ago there was a merchant in Isfahan, and he had a daughter called Roshan ('Bright'). She was his only child and he loved her more than anyone in the world. He had married young and his wife had borne him several children, but they had all died before they could walk. In those days it was common for infants to die, no matter what you did or how well you took care of them. People asked holy men to write special prayers on pieces of paper, covered them with cloth and pinned them on their babies' chests for protection from disease and accident, and they hung amulets round their necks against the evil eye. Sometimes this worked and the babies survived; sometimes it didn't. Roshan was the only one of her father's children to reach adulthood, and her parents doted on her, calling her the light of their eyes.

When Roshan grew up and became a pretty girl of fourteen, it was time for her to get married. They used to say you should marry your daughter as soon as her breasts begin to grow and your son when a dark shadow appears above his upper lip, to keep them out of mischief. Roshan had many suitors and her parents had difficulty choosing the best among them. Finally they accepted the hand of Saeed ('Fortunate'), another Bazaar trader's son, who seemed perfect — handsome, modest and courteous.

After a great wedding feast to which half the Bazaar was invited and where food was distributed among the poor, Roshan was taken to her husband's house in a bridal carriage, followed by three carts full of large ornate chests containing her trousseau.

It was customary for a young couple to live with the husband's parents and for the young bride to learn the ropes from her mother-in-law. In due course the parents would grow old and die, and the son become the head of the household, and so it went on from generation to generation.

Roshan's mother-in-law was a widow and a kind woman. One day she said to Roshan, 'Now that you have been married for a while and learnt to cope with domestic life, I can leave you and go and visit my brother in Shiraz. He is getting old and I want to spend some time with him.'

She packed her bags for a long stay and joined a caravan bound for the South, for Shiraz.

Every morning after her husband left for work, Roshan occupied herself with everyday tasks, visited her family and friends, prepared the evening meal and waited for him to return at dusk. One afternoon when she had finished her work and did not feel like a siesta, she decided to open her chests and look at her beautiful trousseau. As once again she was admiring the turquoise and pearl necklace her mother had given her to wear on special occasions, and her fine silver-and-gold-threaded cashmere brocade to be made into shawls and covers, she heard the sound of scratching on the back door. Who could it be, she wondered.

'Who is it?' she called out, but no answer came. Instead the sound continued as if someone was manipulating the lock and trying to break it and open the door. She felt very scared — all alone in the house, with no one within earshot and no way of defending herself.

As she was pondering what to do, the door opened and a young man stepped in. Roshan saw immediately that he was a burglar, for he looked rough, his feet were wrapped in felt so no one would hear his footsteps and he had a big empty bag which doubtless he planned to fill.

Roshan was terrified, but she managed to control herself and quick as a flash jumped to her feet saying, 'Good afternoon, my dear, dear Uncle! Welcome! Welcome! May my eyes be the mat on which you step! Come in please, I'm so happy to see you! Where have you been all these years? I'm dying to hear all about your travels. We missed you so much at my wedding, especially my mother who kept sighing and saying, "If only my beloved brother was here to share our happiness!" I haven't seen you since I was a child — I bet you don't even recognize me! Had you sent word about your arrival I would have prepared a more worthy welcome, sacrificed a lamb and prepared a banquet for you. As it is, you will have to be content with pot-luck. But you look so tired after your long journey, even though you have sensibly covered your feet with felt, and you must be famished. Please sit down and rest your back against these cushions while I warm some water to wash your weary feet and prepare you a meal.'

Saying this she rushed to the kitchen to get what was needed. The Thief was so flabbergasted by Roshan's welcome and solicitude that he didn't know what to do. He was about to run out and escape when Roshan returned with a pitcher of hot water, a basin, a bar of soap and a towel.

'I know you are exhausted,' she said, 'so I will wash your feet myself', and before the Thief could protest, she sat down and proceeded to unwrap his feet and wash, massage and dry them, as she often did her husband's. She next washed his hands and put henna on both his fingers and toes, saying, 'While you wait for the henna to colour, dearest Uncle, I will fetch your lunch.' Beside its warm, cheerful colour, henna has many medicinal properties which are good for the skin and, when massaged into the soles of the feet, it extracts fatigue and relaxes the body.

The dumbfounded Thief, his hands and feet covered with a thick paste, again wanted to escape but Roshan entered with a tray of food. The Thief was hungry and the delicious aroma of saffron rice and stew, fresh herbs and warm bread weakened his resolve to run away; instead he ate heartily, pondering his next move. Meanwhile Roshan kept up her affectionate talk so as not to let a second of silence make the Thief feel awkward or obliged to respond, telling him how good and diligent her husband was, and how kind and clever was her mother-in-law at teaching her cooking and sewing, and so on.

The Thief decided that, given the circumstances, he should play along with the pretence for a while, and at the first opportunity, steal everything precious in the house and bolt. This plan made him relax and enjoy the *nargileh* (waterpipe, hubble-bubble) Roshan brought him, and he soon dozed off.

That was exactly what Roshan had hoped for — she quietly slipped out of the room, dashed to the neighbours' house and told them what was happening. They all rushed to her house and gave the Thief a thorough beating before throwing him out into the street, half dead.

Everyone admired Roshan's presence of mind and cleverness, and after a while the incident was forgotten. Meanwhile the Thief dragged himself to his home, giving thanks to God for sparing his life. Once he had nursed his bruises, he began to feel very angry at having been fooled by a crafty young girl and he vowed to have his revenge.

Time passed. Roshan's mother-in-law came back from her long journey and one evening as she and Roshan were waiting for Saeed to come home from the Bazaar, they heard a knock on the door.

Who could it be at this hour, they wondered, as they did not expect any guests. When they opened the door they saw two hefty men with three big chests loaded on to a horse-drawn cart.

'We come from Haji Amin's chambers,' they said. 'He sends his greetings and asks if you would be so kind as to keep these chests in your house for a few months while he is travelling abroad. They contain valuables which he is reluctant to leave in his depot, for fear of burglars breaking in.'

Roshan was about to find an excuse and refuse, having a hunch that there was something odd in such a request, but her mother-in-law said, 'Sure! Bring them in and I will show you where to put them.'

She led the men to a back room where their own valuable belongings were stored, and they set down the chests and left.

Once the men had gone, Roshan examined the chests and saw that two of them were padlocked, but the third was not. She went and bought a big padlock, and put it on the third chest so that all three were completely secured.

Now inside each chest was a man, the Thief's accomplices, and their plan was that at night the man in the unlocked chest would get out, open the other two and let out his partners, and the three of them would rob the house clean and escape. But after supper, as soon as everybody had gone to bed, Roshan slithered out of bed without waking her husband, went into the kitchen and boiled a huge vat of oil. She then made a large hole in the lid of each chest and poured the boiling oil into it. The men inside screamed with pain and pleaded with her to spare their lives, but it was too late. After a few minutes Roshan opened the lids only to find that all three thieves were so badly burnt that they had lost consciousness. She dragged them one by one out of the house, locked the door and went back to bed.

In the morning she looked through the window to see if the men were still there in the street where she had left them unconscious, but they had gone. After regaining consciousness they had crawled to the Thief's house and told him the story. The Thief was beside himself with fury and frustration, and cursed the little vixen. He decided that he had to devise a stratagem to kill Roshan and avenge himself and his partners. Otherwise people would gossip, the story would spread that he had been outwitted yet again by a mere woman and he would lose all authority with his minions and colleagues.

Meanwhile Roshan had brought luck to her husband and he was doing so well in his business that he became eligible for *Hajj* (the pilgrimage to Mecca, a compulsory religious duty for the wealthy). In those days the journey was long and hazardous, and it was a man's duty to leave at least one year's living expenses for his family, otherwise his pilgrimage would not be lawful. Roshan prepared her husband's luggage with loving care, making sure that he had everything he needed, and on the day of his departure she accompanied him to the gate of the city where he joined the caravan of pilgrims to the House of God in Mecca.

Barely a month had gone by when news came that during the crossing of the Persian Gulf a sudden and fierce storm had raged in which Saeed's ship had sunk, and the whole caravan had perished. Roshan was disconsolate — still in her teens and already a widow!

What a calamity! For forty days ceremonies of mourning and commemoration continued in the Bazaar and in the bereaved households, after which Roshan returned to her parents' home, as custom required, and her mother-in-law decided to go back to Shiraz and spend the rest of her days with her brother and his family.

During this time the Thief too had done well, and he had accumulated great wealth and gained a high reputation in his profession. But he could not get Roshan out of his mind, and when he heard that she had become a widow and gone back to live with her parents, he devised a sure plan to take revenge for the humiliation he had suffered.

He knew an old crone called Zerang Khanum ('Lady Clever'), who had a reputation as a clever marriage-broker and trader in charms and amulets, and he offered her a deal. She was to make friends with Roshan's mother, insinuate herself into her household and persuade Roshan to accompany her to the mosque, whereupon she would bring her to the Thief's house instead and leave the rest to him. He did not tell her that he intended to kill Roshan; he said that he had fallen head over heels in love with her and wanted to be alone with her for an hour to persuade her to marry him. Zerang Khanum's reward would be a purseful of gold sovereigns.

At first she refused, for she already knew of Roshan and was planning to find her a new husband and collect a big reward from her parents, and she feared that the Thief might rape Roshan, or at least damage her reputation, which together with her widowhood would put her definitely out of the marriage market. The Thief doubled, trebled and finally quadrupled his offer, and Zerang Khanum gave in.

'Leave it to me,' she said, 'but I must warn you that it may take some time.'

The first thing Zerang Khanum did was to rent a room near Roshan's house so as to observe the comings and goings of the household. One morning, after Roshan's father left for work, she knocked on their door and introduced herself as their new neighbour wishing to make their acquaintance. She was welcomed in and offered a cup of tea and sweetmeats, which she refused, saying that she was fasting — even though it was not *Ramadan*.[1] She explained that she was a poor widow who fasted most of the year, spent her days at the mosque praying and lived only to fulfil God's commandments. She had a rosary in her hand and kept turning the beads, invoking God, His Prophet, the Imams and saints, saying that idle tongues and ears were prone to gossip and mischief-making, that it was better to occupy them with invocations and holy thoughts.

Roshan's mother was most impressed with Zerang Khanum's piety and wisdom, and she told her that she would always be welcome in their house.

The old crone thanked her, saying, 'May God's shadow never leave your roof, may He protect you and your pretty daughter from the evil eye', and many other such expressions.

Every day after that she found an excuse to call at Roshan's house. One day she needed a sieve to sift the flour for making bread, another day she had run out of water and wanted to make her ablutions at their pool, yet another day she had made some sweetmeats and brought them a plateful, all the while turning her rosary, whispering prayers and raising her eyes to Heaven in supplication and submission to the Will of God. Before long Roshan's mother, who was as guileless as Zerang was wily, was fooled by her hypocrisy and had made her a bosom friend.

Some months later Roshan's mother decided to go away for a few days to visit her sister, who had recently moved to the other side of town, and she left Roshan in charge of the household.

The very next day Zerang Khanum called at the house with a message from Roshan's mother. She wanted Roshan to join her at once, as her cousin was getting married and the family insisted on her presence at the wedding. They had sent horses and a groom to fetch her, and Zerang Khanum was to accompany her. Sure enough there was a gleaming white mare in front of the house, with a brand new saddle and a liveried groom holding its bridle, and two other bay horses.

Roshan had no idea that her cousin was getting married, but she was delighted at the news, and anyway in those days the young obeyed their elders and her mother's wish was her command. So she attired herself in fine clothes, perfumed herself with attar of rose, mounted the mare and rode off with Zerang Khanum and the groom.

They rode and rode until they reached the gate of the city and still there was no sign of her aunt's house.

'How far is my aunt's new house?' asked Roshan and the old crone answered, 'Not far, just a furlong or two further.'

After a while they reached the outer walls of a large domain. Presently the groom stopped the horses in front of a massive door, opened it with a huge key and led them into a beautiful garden, with tall cypresses and orange groves and fountains, and a lovely house at the end of a shaded alley. Roshan expected the house to be teeming with guests, ringing with music and gaiety, but instead she found it deserted, dark and silent. Where was the wedding? She turned to ask the servant, but he had simply vanished. Zerang Khanum told her to wait there while she went and found out what was happening and where her mother was — perhaps the party was in another house nearby.

As soon as Zerang left the room, Roshan realized that it might be the Thief who had cooked up the whole story of the cousin's wedding to trap her and that the old crone might be his accomplice.

Unlike her naive mother, Roshan had always been suspicious of Zerang, finding her religious zeal too excessive to be genuine.

But what could she do now? This time she thought she was done for. She ran to the door, but Zerang had locked it behind her, and the windows were fastened and barred as well. She looked around the room — it was sumptuously furnished and there was a glass display case containing magnificent pieces of jewellery and some jewel-encrusted daggers.

The only possible escape route was the fanlight above the door. She broke the glass of the display cabinet, filled her pockets with the best pieces of jewellery and took a couple of daggers and stuck them into her belt. Then she pushed a chest to the door, climbed on it, broke the fanlight and managed to squeeze out and jump down, covered with cuts and bruises.

She looked around, the garden was empty, and she ran to the shed, mounted the white mare and quietly rode out to the gate. It was secured with a heavy padlock the size of a lion's paw! But the horse, as if used to another route, trotted along the wall to a small door hidden behind an old plane tree, which it pushed open with its head, and Roshan found herself outside, not far from the highway.

At the touch of the spur the horse started galloping away like a bird on the wing and soon they reached the city gates. What a relief! Roshan tethered the horse to a tree in the main square and ran to her house, knowing that the Thief would follow, recognize his white mare and take her away.

Now let me tell you about the Thief. He was hiding in a gazebo at the far side of the garden, sharpening a dagger on a whetstone, intending to kill the impertinent minx who had dared to pitch herself against *him* — the most skilful burglar in the land, a burglar who had never been caught. Armed with his weapon, he went to the house, where Roshan was supposed to be waiting, unaware of what was in store for her. He unlocked the door and entered, but lo! the bird had flown! Once again Roshan had 'laughed at his beard' — once again she had outwitted him. What is more, she had broken the glass cabinet and taken his most precious jewels and best daggers. He was beside himself with rage.

'Where is the little harpy?' he yelled and called for Zerang Khanum. She rushed in and, amazed at what she found, told him that she had locked the door as instructed and that there was nothing more she could have done. She was as angry with Roshan as he was.

Noticing the broken fanlight they realized how she had escaped, and when they found out that the horse had gone too they pieced together her movements. Within minutes the Thief galloped off in pursuit, but all he found in the town was the white mare, tethered to a tree in the main square. Once again his scheme had failed. He raved and moaned and swore the mother of all revenges, even if it cost him the rest of his fortune.

Back home and glad to have escaped with her life, Roshan said nothing about her latest adventure to anyone. After a few days her mother came back and immediately sent for her friend Zerang Khanum, only to be told that the old woman had gone no one knew where. She assumed that she had gone on pilgrimage, being so godly and observant, and would return in due course.

As for the Thief, he devised a long-term plan to lay his hand on Roshan: he gave up burglary, assumed the grand name of Haji Bozorg (Great Haji) and became a goldsmith, with a brand new shop in the Goldsmiths' Bazaar. What with his trimmed beard and moustachios that offset his ruddy cheeks, his silk shirt and paisley coat and ambergris rosary, nobody could guess that he was the wild, intrepid Thief, the account of whose exploits sent shivers through the population.

One day Roshan went to the Bazaar with her mother and noticed the new shop, all a-glitter with gold jewellery and ornaments, and sitting inside, the merchant himself. As soon as she saw his face, she recognized him. 'My God!' she whispered under her breath. 'The Thief!' She remembered the miseries he had put her through and smiled with satisfaction at having outwitted him. Could it be that he really had reformed and taken to the straight and narrow, she wondered.

Pretending that she had not recognized him, she entered the shop and examined several bracelets and necklaces, asking their price and bargaining, gently flirting with the Haji. She said that she would come back another day with her mother to choose a present for a friend, and left the shop. The Thief rubbed his hands with glee that Roshan had not recognized him and that the first stage of his plan had worked.

It was not easy in those days for a widow, even a young and pretty one, to find a second husband. Who wanted a girl who was not a virgin? She was considered 'damaged goods', a second-hand or hand-me-down garment. Her only hope was an old man or an invalid, or a widower who needed someone to look after him and his children. But Roshan was resourceful as well as pretty and vivacious, so she had several good offers, but she turned them all down, to the consternation of her parents, saying that she was not yet ready, that she was still mourning her Saeed.

'A woman must be married,' her mother told her, 'otherwise who will protect her after her parents are gone?'

Roshan tried to soothe her anxieties, telling her to trust in Providence and that one day someone suitable would turn up.

One day Haji Bozorg, the erstwhile Thief and new goldsmith, sent a well-known go-between to ask for Roshan's hand. Her parents were overjoyed — surely the young merchant was one of the best catches in town, healthy and rich, and by good fortune he had set his heart on their daughter. They were amazed when Roshan refused.

'Don't kick your luck,' her mother said. 'You had one good husband, and now God is putting another one your way — why say no?'

As she would not listen to their reasoning, her father finally put his foot down and said that, whether she liked it or not, he had accepted the young merchant's offer.

There was nothing for it but to submit, and soon marriage preparations got under way. As the wedding day approached, the Thief was sizzling with excitement, unable to hide his joy, to the amusement of his colleagues in the Bazaar who had never seen a young man so happy at the prospect of matrimony.

As for Roshan, she seemed calm, going about arranging her trousseau and getting ready for the festivities. But secretly she was making sure that whatever scheme the Thief had concocted, she would be able to unravel it. She secretly bought a goat skin, filled it with a most delicious concoction of *shireh* (a kind of molasses) and fruit juice, and used it as the bust of a dummy, to which she added wax arms and legs, and a wax head with the face painted in her own likeness. She had her wedding dress and veil duplicated and dressed the dummy exactly like herself. On her wedding night she put it in a bag and took it with her trousseau to her husband's house.

She was amazed at the magnificent reception. The Thief had not stinted on anything — lanterns hung from trees, goldfish swam in fountains, and a lavish banquet was served to men and women in their separate quarters, while musicians played and dancers whirled and singers sang love songs to melt the heart. A great time was had by all until late in the night.

Then the guests departed, saying, 'May God keep your table always covered with food; may health and prosperity never leave your house', and so on.

As custom had it, the bride was taken to her bridal room by the women of her family and installed on the bridal bed to await her husband. They kissed her goodbye, wished her long life and happiness and many children, and left.

As soon as she was alone in the bridal room, Roshan took the dummy out of the bag and installed it in her place on the dais while she herself hid behind a curtain. She had tied a string to the dummy's neck, and whenever she pulled it the dummy nodded, as if to say 'Yes'.

Presently the groom entered the room, all dressed up in fine clothes, his dark hair and beard smooth with scented oil, his eyes two gleaming pieces of ebony. There on the bed was his young bride, by now twenty years old, ravishing in white satin and lace, with a purple chiffon veil over her head and shoulders, which he was supposed to lift and see her face for the first time, as custom had it. The soft light of the candles enhanced her beauty, and he took her lowered eyes for bridal modesty.

'So, here we are at last!' he chuckled. 'We will see how you can escape me this time, you crafty little witch! You thought you were clever, did you?'

Roshan pulled the string from behind the curtain and the dummy nodded 'Yes'.

This cheekiness incensed the Thief and he yelled, 'Nobody has ever caught or outwitted me, you hear?'

Roshan pulled the string and the dummy nodded 'Yes' again.

'Did you really think I wanted to marry a woman with a tongue like yours?'

'Yes,' indicated the dummy, making him more and more angry.

'Why don't you talk? What happened to your sweet-talking, the clever babble you used the first time I came to your house? I will show you how women like you should be treated!'

Saying this he drew his dagger, lunged forward and plunged it into the dummy's heart. Clear red liquid spurted out of the dummy and spread all over the dais. The Thief cupped his hand to collect and drink Roshan's blood so that at last his thirst for vengeance could be sated. As soon as his lips touched the liquid and he felt its sweet taste he stopped. It was not blood, it was nectar! The drink of the Gods! As sweet as the water of *Kowthar*² in Paradise! In all his life he had never tasted a more delicious beverage and suddenly he realized what he had done.

He threw himself over the dummy and began to lament. 'Oh my beloved! What have I done? Your blood is as sweet as yourself! I fell in love with you the minute I saw you! But what hope had I, a wretched burglar, of winning you? Oh, would that you had killed me there and then! Oh God! Oh Prophet! Oh Imams! Help me! What have I done?'

He wept and beat his chest, as the dummy collapsed on its side, seemingly dead. He could not bear the pain of remorse any longer and sitting up he sobbed, 'I cannot live without you, my Roshan, "light of my eyes", I am going to join you in the next world.'

Saying this he lifted the dagger to stab his own heart and die beside the woman he loved, but at that very moment Roshan rushed forward and caught his wrist.

'What would happen to your bride if you died?' she said laughing. 'Do you want to make me a widow for a second time?'

When the Thief saw that Roshan was alive and well, he threw himself at her feet and begged her forgiveness for all the troubles he had caused her. It had all been because he loved her and could not have her, he explained. She lifted him gently and kissed him tenderly, and they spent the night in the ecstasy of love until dawn.

The Thief remained the honoured merchant in the Bazaar that people thought he was and his business throve. He made amends for his past misdeeds by giving generously to the poor and needy, always thanking God for bestowing upon him the greatest of blessings — a good woman. The Thief and his clever wife lived happily ever after and had many children.

The Talking Skull

There was one and there was none/Except for God there was no one.

T here was once a prosperous merchant in Khorassan who lived in the blessed city of Meshed. Having reached a certain age and amassed a great fortune, he decided to satisfy his wanderlust and undertake a long journey around the world. It was a dream he had nurtured for many years: to go west and visit the Holy Cities of Mecca and Medina, then take the boat across the Sea of Arabia to Farangistan and spend some time getting to know the people and their customs, then sail across the Indian Ocean to Zanzibar and see its famous markets, and finally travel through India and China before returning home. He would bring back new and unusual merchandise from all these exotic lands and sell them to his own community.

This adventurous merchant had a wife, and a daughter called Akhtar ('Star'), who was approaching puberty. One day he told them about his plans and urged them to be careful in his absence, preserve their honour and do nothing to damage the reputation for righteousness he had acquired over long years of honest trading.

It was customary that when the head of the family went abroad, or died, his nearest male relative took care of his household. So on the eve of his departure the Merchant went to visit his brother to say goodbye and ask him to keep an eye on his family. His brother lived in a village a few miles from the city, and on his way back home the Merchant took a short-cut across a stretch of the desert.

As he was walking and pondering his forthcoming journey, he heard a voice calling his name. He stopped and looked around, but he saw no one, just the empty, silent wilderness. He resumed his walk, thinking that perhaps his imagination was teasing him, but again he heard the voice, this time saying, 'I have killed forty men and, before I have finished, I shall kill one more.'

Following the direction of the voice he noticed to his utter astonishment that the voice came from a skull, lying on the stony ground. So awe-stricken was he at such an extraordinary phenomenon that he was nailed to the spot, wondering whether he was dreaming or hallucinating, for how could a skull, buried in the desert perhaps for hundreds of years, speak like a living man? As if reading his mind, the skull repeated what it had said and added, 'Don't doubt what I say, for I tell the truth.'

What should he do, he wondered. Instead of reciting a prayer and burying the skull, he picked it up, wrapped it in a handkerchief and took it home. He found a pestle and mortar in the kitchen, went to his room, locked the door and pounded the skull into a fine white powder. He poured the powder into a glass jar and screwed on the top firmly, saying sarcastically, 'Now we shall see if you can scare people with your nimble tongue, or kill one more man!'

Old houses used to have several niches in every room for putting lamps and ornaments in, much as today they have shelves and mantelpieces, and the Merchant left the jar in the highest niche in the sitting-room, where it would be secure. The next morning he told his wife and daughter that on no account should they touch the jar, or let anyone else have access to it, for it contained *zahr-e-halal*, the deadliest poison in the world, which killed instantly anyone who came into contact with it. He then kissed them goodbye and embarked upon his long journey.

A few months later, the Merchant's daughter began to menstruate. It was not uncommon for this event to be accompanied with pain, especially before a woman got married and had children. Menstruation was not like today, when modern doctors can give you some pill or other to help you get through it; in those days you just put up with it until you married and had a baby, and with any luck it stopped bothering you. In the case of the Merchant's daughter the pain was extreme, and the poor girl went through several days of excruciating suffering. Every month as her period approached she anticipated the agony, and gradually became so unhappy that she decided to take her own life.

One day when the pain became unbearable she recalled what her father had said about the deadly poison in the jar. She took it down, swallowed a spoonful and lay down waiting for death to come and release her. Instead the pain stopped at once and a feeling of well-being spread through her whole body. She was relieved and wondered why her father had said that if anybody so much as touched the powder he or she would drop dead. Perhaps it was just his way of testing their obedience.

The following month terrible pains again accompanied the approach of her period and again Akhtar took a teaspoonful of the powder, with the same result — instant relief and happiness.

Inevitably there came a day when the jar was empty and she panicked at the thought of her calvary returning, but at the expected date her period did not happen; instead her tummy began to swell, as if she were pregnant. After a few months her mother, noticing the bulge of her stomach, beat her chest in despair, certain that her daughter had been seduced by some knave and lost her virginity. How could she answer her husband when he returned? He would accuse her of being a careless mother, unable to safeguard her daughter's honour, and he would punish her, and who would blame him?

She confronted her daughter and demanded to know the name of the miscreant, but the young girl swore that she was innocent, that no man had been near her, and she told her about her attempted suicide with the poison powder, showing her the empty jar. A midwife was called in to examine her, and she confirmed that indeed Akhtar was a virgin, that no man had been close to her. Honour was saved! The news spread through the town that a virgin birth was imminent, and when in due course the baby was born they called him Khodadad, which means 'God-given', and they treated the baby as a gift from Heaven. In those days people believed in miracles and sometimes, indeed, they happened; this was one of them.

Time passed. The child grew up into a delightful little boy, then a beautiful youth, charming and clever and helpful, loved by the whole community. Above all he had the rare gift of clairvoyance, as if he had access to *Alam-e-Gheib* — the Occult World.

Meanwhile the Merchant had travelled all over the world, East and West, and one day he sent news that at last he was returning home. The whole town went mad; the Bazaar was flood-lit and decorated, and several lambs were slaughtered at different points on his way from the city gate to his house. As custom required, he held court in his *birouni* (the men's quarters of a large house) for seven days, during which all the notables of the town came to pay their respects and hear about his adventures. He hardly had any time for his family, the house being always full of visitors, relations, colleagues and friends. Eventually the excitement of his return subsided and he was glad to be at last with his wife and daughter.

Upon entering the sitting-room in the *andaroun* (the women's quarters) he saw a most attractive young man seated beside his daughter, holding her hand and kissing her face. As soon as they noticed him they rushed forward to greet him, and before he had time to ask any questions about the young man, his daughter told him the whole story — her taking the poison, her pregnancy and childbirth. Finally, pointing to her son, she said, 'Here is your grandson and heir.'

The young man bowed and kissed his grandfather's hand, but instead of expressing joy, the Merchant went pale, collapsed on to a mattress and sank into the deepest despondency. Nobody could understand why, since none of them knew anything about the talking skull, but he himself remembered the skull's words: 'I have killed forty men and, before I have finished, I shall kill one more.' Never mind the forty, they were in the past, but who would that last, forty-first man be, he wondered. Would his grandson become a murderer? Would he perhaps even kill him, his own grandfather, to steal his wealth? His soul was in torment, while his wife was bewildered and his daughter felt deeply hurt at his lack of enthusiasm for such a perfect heir.

Only his grandson, Khodadad himself, showed no surprise. He told them not to worry, that years of travelling had taken their toll, and that in time his grandfather would settle down and become himself again. In the meantime he would take care of the business. He opened the shop and began to sell all the exotic merchandise his grandfather had brought back from all over the world.

The news spread that the Merchant's shop had reopened and was full of the most desirable goods from Farangistan as well as the Orient. People rushed from all over the region to see his display, and were dazzled, not only by the novelty of the merchandise, but even more by the radiant beauty of the young man who was selling it. So after their purchases they lingered for a long time just to gaze at him, unable to tear themselves away. Surely Khodadad was a new Joseph and the women clients so many Zuleikhas who had lost their reason for the love of him.

Soon the news of Khodadad's good looks and bewitching charm spread far and wide, and eventually reached even the Royal Palace. Now the King had a daughter, Princess Shahnaz, who was famous throughout the land for her beauty and accomplishments; they said that she was 'fair and fresh like a flower, learned and wise like a savant'. Shahnaz was intrigued by what she heard about Khodadad and one day she sent her personal hand-maid, who was also her confidante and constant companion, to see the young man for herself and bring back her impressions. As soon as the maid set eyes on Khodadad, she fainted, struck down by his radiant beauty, just like the women in Potiphar's Palace upon seeing Joseph. When she came to, she bought some trifle and stood back from the other buyers to feast her eyes on Khodadad for a few minutes longer. The cry of the *Muezzin* calling the faithful to the midday prayer brought her out of her reverie and she realized that she was late. How could she be forgiven for her delay? She had two legs and borrowed two more, as they say, and running as fast as a panther, reached the Shah's Palace and rushed to Shahnaz's apartments, flushed and breathless.

The Princess asked her what had kept her so long, and she replied, 'If I went in the morning and returned at noon, you will stay for ever and ever and never return', and she proceeded to describe Khodadad's beauty and charm, his gentle manners and mellifluous voice, until the Princess said 'Enough!' and forgave her for being late.

Tickled by curiosity, Princess Shahnaz resolved to have a look at this wonder-boy herself, believing herself immune to such spells. The next morning she dressed as a lady of means but without any sign of royalty, slipped out of the Palace through a secret door to avoid the guards, and went to Khodadad's shop. This was before photographs made everybody's face familiar to the whole world. There were of course portraits of kings and princes and vizirs, but they were rare and few people saw them. So nobody in the crowd recognized the Princess and anyway they were all too enchanted by Khodadad to look at anyone else.

Upon setting eyes on this new Joseph, Shahnaz too was dazzled by some uncanny quality in his aspect, but she controlled herself, bought a few yards of a particularly lovely silk and paid him double the price. Khodadad was an honest merchant and insisted on giving back the extra money, impressing the Princess with his decency and pride.

Now, my dear, hold on to the thread of the story while I tell you about the King. He was a just and benevolent ruler, and he cared about his people's well-being. To make sure that the population was content, that justice was done and that no one in a position of power bullied his subordinates, he and his Vizir periodically disguised themselves as wandering dervishes and roamed the streets at night, listening to people talk, asking questions, gathering information. People often pour out their hearts to strangers more readily than to those they know, thinking that the strangers will be gone soon without spreading their secrets. So they spoke freely to these two dervishes passing through their city, believing them to be men of God, detached from the world and not likely to betray them or cause them trouble. In this way the Shah could render justice and keep his people content. But he himself had a sorrow: he longed for his only daughter to get married and produce an heir to the throne, but she always found fault with her suitors and turned them down, telling her father that she was satisfied living with him and needed no other man in her life.

One evening, just before closing time, the King and his Vizir were walking through the Bazaar in disguise, mingling with the crowd. They came near a shop where they saw a large glass basin full of water in which swam two goldfish, one male and the other female. As they watched they noticed that the male was pursuing the female round and round the basin, while the female dodged and dived and twisted to escape him. After a while, tired of resistance, the female gave in and they entwined. The King laughed. The Vizir was a shrewd man, and he suggested they buy the glass basin with the goldfish and take it home to Princess Shahnaz as a present — sharp as she was, she would immediately understand this clue to the natural order of things and she would accept one of her many suitors. The King agreed.

Back at the Palace the King sent word to his daughter that he wished to visit her in her apartments and give her a present. Shahnaz was delighted with the two goldfish. Soon she saw how doggedly the male pursued the female, no matter how coquettishly she slipped away and played hard-to-get, until she finally relented. The King smiled at his daughter and suggested that perhaps she too should submit to Nature's law and choose a mate. Instead of agreeing with her father as she usually did, or at least finding some excuse, the Princess became very angry: she hit her father on the head with her clenched fist, saying, 'Idiot! What is already there is enough!' and ran out of the room.

Well! You can imagine the wrath of the King! His dutiful, loving daughter, the joy of his life, had dared to strike him in front of his Vizir! This was unimaginable, and he had no choice but to order her immediate arrest and execution, otherwise his authority would be lost forever. He summoned his Executioner, who was always at hand with his sharpened sword, ready to chop off the head of anyone who incurred the King's displeasure, and told him to stand and wait for his orders.

Meanwhile the Princess had escaped, and while the flunkies searched for her all over the Palace, the King's anger subsided. Shahnaz was his only child and he loved her with all his heart; how could he live without her? She had always been the most affectionate and respectful of daughters — what had come over her all of a sudden? She must have had some good reason to behave as she had, he was certain, but he could not think of any. At the same time if he forgave her his authority, on which his whole kingdom was built, would be impaired irrevocably. He was in a terrible conundrum. Besides what had she meant by 'What is already there is enough!', he wondered. Surely it was a riddle whose solution would shed light on her outburst, and perhaps enable him to spare her life.

He asked his Vizir for an explanation. The Vizir pondered a while, but confessed that, for the life of him, he too was unable to understand either her behaviour or the meaning of her words.

Frustrated and desperate, the King transferred his anger to his Vizir and told him that he had forty days in which to solve the riddle, failing which he would be executed in the Public Square. The King was convinced that his canny Vizir would find a solution that would save his beloved daughter's life and re-establish his absolute authority, and he felt somewhat calmer.

The wretched Vizir called upon all the wise men and women of the kingdom — philosophers and divines and white-beards of all persuasions — but none could solve the riddle. Thirty-nine days passed and still no answer was found. The following day the Vizir would be called to the Court, then dragged to the Public Square and beheaded in front of the whole town. He was in despair and so were his family and household.

Now the Vizir, too, had a pretty and resourceful daughter, called Mahnaz ('Caressed by the Moon'), whom he loved dearly, and she suggested that they appeal to Khodadad, for everyone swore by his clairvoyance and his knowledge of the Occult World. At first the Vizir was doubtful, saying that where the wisest men had failed a mere youth could not possibly succeed, but his daughter insisted that this was their last chance and that they might as well take it — what could they lose at this eleventh hour?

It was late at night when the Vizir reached Khodadad's house and knocked on the door. Khodadad opened it and greeted the Vizir, expressing no surprise at his visit, as if he had been expecting him. 'I know what you want,' he said. 'Go back home and sleep, and I will see you first thing in the morning.'

Naturally the Vizir and his family did not have a wink of sleep. At dawn, as the cock crowed and the sun appeared on the crest of the distant mountains, there was a knock on the door.

'Heavens!' gasped the Vizir and his heart sank, thinking that it was the King's emissaries who had come to fetch him. But it was Khodadad — he had kept his promise! When a few minutes later the Shah's men arrived to take the Vizir, Khodadad went with him.

At the Palace the King was waiting in his throne-room. 'Well, what have you brought me?' he asked his Vizir. 'Have you solved the riddle of my daughter's words?'

The Vizir pointed to Khodadad, saying, 'Your Majesty! I believe this young man has the answer.'

The King was struck by Khodadad's radiant countenance and felt relieved that the matter could be settled without him losing either his beloved daughter or his loyal Vizir.

Khodadad asked for Shahnaz's mother, the Queen, to be present, and together with the King and the Vizir they went to

Shahnaz's apartments. The Princess was not there and no one knew where she was. But on the ledge above the door of her room, hidden from view, he found a key. He used it to open a small safe, made of mother-of-pearl and gold, which was the most beautiful ornament in the room. Inside the box was a bunch of keys. Khodadad took it and with the first key he opened a secret door behind a heavy curtain which led into a large room. At the end of this room another hidden door opened into a second room, and another and another ... each key fitting into the lock of a hidden door, until they reached the end of the building where they found a little closet. There Khodadad raked the floor and a big iron ring appeared attached to a heavy stone. He pulled the ring and removed the stone to reveal a ladder going down into a dark cellar. He asked the others to wait while he went down to reconnoitre, saying that if he had not returned by noon they would know that he had run into trouble and should come to his rescue.

Holding a candle to light his way, Khodadad descended into the cellar, at the end of which he saw the outline of a door. He pushed it open and stepped into a new world: a most luxurious palace, grander than the Padishah's. He tiptoed along the corridors and looked through the keyholes to see inside the rooms. All were brightly lit and splendidly furnished — silk carpets and magnificent tapestries and ornaments, mirrors and chandeliers. In each room was a golden dais covered with rugs and cushions, and sitting on each dais were two sturdy young men playing chess, completely absorbed in the game.

He pushed the first door gently and went in. Startled by his sudden entrance, the two players jumped up and drew their swords. Khodadad pacified them, saying that he meant no harm, and he asked them who they were and how they had come to be there. They told him their stories.

'Looking at our attires you may think that we are courtiers to the manner born,' they began, 'but in truth we are highwaymen. We started life as orphans and grew up in dire poverty. We saw no future except drudgery and deprivation, so we escaped and took to the highway, robbing caravans and travellers, and living in the woods. But in the end the Law caught up with us — we were taken to the *Qazi* (religious judge), tried and condemned to death.

'But just before we were led to the place of execution in the Public Square, a eunuch appeared out of nowhere. No one knew him, but he paid a rich ransom for our heads, with the guarantee that we would leave the country at once and never return. Over-joyed to be reprieved, we put ourselves at the disposal of our saviour, pledging to be his devoted servants forever and asking him to do with us whatever he wished. Whereupon he blindfolded us and took us on what seemed a long journey. When he removed the cloth from our eyes, we found ourselves in this magnificent palace, wondering whether we had indeed been hanged and by the Grace of God gone to Paradise. Only the presence of the Eunuch brought us back to reality. He had us groomed, taught us courtly manners, and when he thought we were truly transformed into gentlemen, he left us, saying, "Soon all will become clear to you."

'That night at the stroke of midnight a Lady, as beautiful as the full moon, came to see us. She asked us to play a game of chess, and took the winner to spend the night with her. We do not know who she is, but we live in anticipation of her visits and we play chess, hoping to improve our chances of winning, for one minute in her arms is an eternity of ecstasy.'

Having told Khodadad their story, the two young men added that although they were not allowed to leave the underground palace, they were very happy, since the young Lady was the most delightful companion, with boundless treasures of knowledge and pleasure, and that nowhere in the world could they find her match.

But Khodadad had trespassed into their domain and learnt their secret, so they had no choice but to kill him.

'It is an order from our Lady herself, that any intruder should be put to the sword at once,' they said, 'otherwise her secret will be divulged and she will be disgraced.'

Khodadad promised not to utter a word to anyone if they spared his life and allowed him to leave, but they refused. At this, they tried to grab Khodadad and kill him, but quick as an arrow he stepped back, turned round and jumped on to the dais which the bandits had vacated in pursuit of him. With the advantage of height, he fought them with all his might, a sword in one hand and a dagger in the other, and he succeeded in killing them both. He then cut off their ears as trophies and tiptoed to the next room.

Here again two hefty youths were playing chess and the same scene was repeated. In every room Khodadad was set upon by two young men determined to kill him; he would plead for his life, and when they refused to spare it, he managed to dispatch them both, until forty in all were dead. He took a cushion cover which he filled with his trophies, forty pairs of ears, and went back through the rooms and the hidden doors until he reached the cellar and the ladder.

Meanwhile the King, his Queen and Vizir were waiting impatiently for Khodadad, counting the minutes and getting more and more anxious, wondering what to do if he failed to return. As for Princess Shahnaz, she was back in her apartments with her maid and none too worried about the outcome. She was certain that should Khodadad manage to find her secret palace, he would be killed instantly by the very first of her forty lovers. Were they not robust highwaymen used to wielding a sword? The same fate would meet anyone else the King would send to find Khodadad.

The King was standing by the window, his eyes glued to the sundial in the garden, which finally indicated noon. Time was up and no sign of Khodadad, but as the King looked anxiously at his Vizir, they heard steps treading on the ladder and presently Khodadad emerged, carrying a bag on his shoulders.

After describing all that had happened to him since he had left them, he opened the bag and put the ears at the Shah's feet, saying, 'Here is the solution to the riddle. When the Princess said "Idiot! What is already there is enough!", she meant that she already had all these lovers and did not need any other man, and that if you had not guessed this, you were not of sound mind.'

At this point a voice from the back shouted 'Liar!' It was the Eunuch. He jumped from behind a curtain, and before anyone could stop him he lunged forward to thrust his poisoned dagger into Khodadad's chest. But lo! the dagger bent like rubber and fell from his hand. The Eunuch pulled out another dagger from his cummerbund and attacked Khodadad again, this time aiming for his throat, but the weapon fell from his hand once more. In the end it was Khodadad who struck his unexpected enemy a fatal blow, and the Eunuch fell at his feet lifeless. The King ordered that the heads of all forty-one bandits be cut off and exhibited at the gates of the city, as a warning to all evil-doers.

When they brought the news to Khodadad's grandfather that his grandson had defeated and beheaded forty-one rascals on behalf of the King, he sighed with relief. At last the talking skull's prophesy had been fulfilled: 'I have killed forty men and, before I have finished, I will kill one more', and behold, here were forty-one heads!

The King was so pleased with the outcome of the events that he reinstated his Vizir and forgave his daughter, provided she promised to lead a virtuous life from then on and to marry within two years. Shahnaz fell down and kissed her father's feet, pledging to be worthy of his forgiveness.

Now Shahnaz, who was already smitten with Khodadad, sensing that in him she had at last found a man worthy of her love and trust, resolved to win his heart. She summoned Khodadad to her palace for a private audience. He could not refuse, but he was determined to resist Shahnaz's charm. She told him that she had taken those lovers because she had found none of her suitors worthy of her heart. They were moved by ambition and wanted to be the King's son-in-law and heir, while the bandits whose lives she had saved loved her without knowing who she was and wanted nothing more than what she gave them.

Khodadad said that he believed her, but that he in turn had a test she had to pass before he consented to marry her.

'What is it?' she asked. 'Tell me, for if you ask for my life I will lay it at your feet.'

Khodadad said that first she had to prove her sincerity and expiate her sins by spending two whole years in prayer and fasting. She must also give her weight in gold to the poor. After that he would see.

Shahnaz agreed. For the love of Khodadad she became the most virtuous of women and all the wealth and intelligence she had put into her life of pleasure she now devoted to the service of the needy.

At the end of only one year Khodadad relented. As for the King, not only did he consent to the match, but he was ecstatic at her daughter's choice, for he knew that in Khodadad he had found a paragon of virtue, and that when the time came for him to leave this world his kingdom would be in safe hands.

Princess Shahnaz and Khodadad were married with pomp and ceremony. A thousand weights of rice and fruit were used for the wedding 'Jewelled pilau'[1] to be distributed among the population. Everybody prayed for the happiness and longevity of the newly weds.

In time the old King died, happy that his kingdom would be run by a just and capable man. Khodadad's *barakat* (divine blessing) spread over the country, and a period of prosperity and justice was enjoyed by all the people.

The Magic Saucepan and the
Piece of Lamb's Tail

There was one and there was none/Except for God there was no one.

Once upon a time there was a widow in Rasht who had fallen on hard times and become very poor. She had a son called Sadeq ('Truthful') whom she loved with all her heart. He was a good boy, gentle and helpful to others, though somewhat ingenuous and gullible. He was willing to work, but he could not find a job. Hard as he tried, he could find nothing, either in his own village or in any other village round about.

One day his mother said to him that they had nothing left to pawn or sell, and no money to buy even a loaf of bread. Her son replied that the only way they could secure a modest income was for him to start a small business of his own, buying and selling everyday essentials to the villagers. His mother agreed, but where could they find the initial capital?

'I have thought of that,' said Sadeq. 'I have borrowed one *qaran* (a shilling) from our good neighbours, and I intend to buy some *donbeh* (lamb tail-fat)[1] which I can sell for two shillings, and go on from there.'

Sadeq's mother was relieved — at last she could see an end to their abject poverty and who knows? Perhaps her son would build up a good business and gradually become a respectable merchant, even go to Mecca and become a *Haji*. With this hope she said goodbye to her son and sent him off to buy his piece of *donbeh*.

Sadeq went to the village butcher and with his *qaran* bought a big chunk of tail-fat, put it on a tray and started walking in the little Bazaar chanting, 'Come and buy my delicious *donbeh* and add succulence to your soup. Come and see what pure fresh lamb-fat I have', and so on. But at the very instant that a client approached to examine and buy a slice of his fat, a crow swooped down, grabbed the whole piece of fat in his beak and flew off.

Sadeq ran after the bird as fast as he could, but it was high in the sky and he had no way of catching it. He was desperate and started shouting at the bird, 'Give me back my *donbeh* or my money, you merciless bird!' but the crow paid no attention; it kept on flapping its wings, the lamb tail-fat dangling from its beak, while Sadeq raced after it, pleading and invoking God and His Prophet.

After a while, what with hunger and struggling hard to keep pace with the bird, his eyes fastened longingly on his *donbeh*, Sadeq became exhausted. Breathless, he was about to stop and give up in despair when suddenly the crow dived down in front of him and disappeared into a well at the side of a field.

Sadeq looked inside the well, but all he could see was a dark, deep shaft with no end in sight, as if a dragon had dug a hole to the centre of the earth. He sat on the border and began to cry, thinking of his hungry mother and the money he owed to the neighbours. 'Give me back my *donbeh* or my *qaran* you merciless bird!' he lamented.

He was struck dumb when out of the well came a hand holding a silver saucepan, with a spoon and a crystal bowl in it. Sadeq was astonished; he thought this was an illusion, a trick played by his empty stomach. Nevertheless he grabbed the saucepan, and immediately the hand vanished and he heard a voice coming from the bottom of the well saying, 'Whenever you want to eat and drink, drum the saucepan with the spoon and say the name of a foodstuff like, "Saffron-rice with stew, saffron-rice with stew", and tap the bowl and say something like, "Spring water and sherbet, spring water and sherbet".'

What was the meaning of this wonder? Was it a trap? Would he be struck down if he said the words? Sadeq was afraid, but hunger gnawed at his stomach and he decided to try, come what may. He picked up the empty saucepan and drummed it with the spoon, repeating, 'Saffron-rice with lamb stew! Saffron-rice with lamb stew!' And lo! the saucepan filled up with steaming-hot rice flavoured with saffron and topped with lamb stew. He took a spoonful — it was the most delicious food he had ever tasted.

Then he tapped the crystal bowl with the silver spoon and said, 'Orange sherbet! Orange sherbet', and it filled with a cool liquid the colour of sunflowers and the smell of orange-blossom. He drank it and praised God for the miracle, put his precious new possessions in his bag and ran home to his mother.

When she saw the silver saucepan and spoon, and heard Sadeq's amazing tale, she could not believe it, but she too was hungry, and she asked him to try again — perhaps the miracle would be repeated. Sadeq stirred the spoon in the saucepan, this time asking for his mother's favourite dish: 'Saffron-rice with aubergine and lamb stew! Saffron-rice with aubergine and lamb stew!', and once again the saucepan filled with scrumptious food, which his mother feasted on with relish.

Well, the magic saucepan became their source of income. Every day at lunchtime Sadeq produced quantities of various delicious dishes and sherbets which he carried to the Bazaar and sold from a makeshift stall. Soon the whole population knew that Sadeq provided the best lunch in town at a reasonable price and everybody rushed to buy from him, tradesmen and shoppers alike. After a few months he had accumulated enough money to acquire a shop in a prominent spot at the crossroads of two major alleys in the Bazaar, and his business flourished. His food was better and cheaper than what was on offer in other restaurants, who lost some of their clients to him, and it was not long before Sadeq became a very rich man. He had a palatial residence built and filled it with the best furniture and ornaments money could buy. Round about it was a garden with flowers and trees and fountains and pools.

His mother was satisfied; she prayed every day and thanked God for their good fortune. But Sadeq was a young man and he harboured greater ambitions. Once a man's belly is full, what does he think about? A wife! So one day he broached the subject with his mother. She was delighted and she mentioned a couple of suitable young girls she knew in the neighbourhood, but Sadeq had higher aspirations. He had once caught a glimpse of the Padishah's daughter, Princess Dorna ('Pearl-like'), as she was driving through the city in her carriage, and he had fallen head over heels in love with her. Now that he was a rich, respectable businessman, he could try his luck and ask the King for her hand.

His mother thought it was a foolish idea, an impossible dream, and she tried to reason with him, saying that too lofty an ambition often led to disappointment and that a more modest girl would be better for him, but Sadeq had lost his heart to the Princess and nothing could dissuade him. 'Either she will be mine or I shall remain celibate for the rest of my life,' he vowed. His mother gave in and suggested that first they invite the Padishah and his Court to dinner to assess Sadeq's chances.

The news of Sadeq's thriving business had reached the Royal Palace, and the King, always glad to hear success stories about his subjects, accepted the invitation. On the appointed evening the Padishah, accompanied by his Grand Vizir and other eminent courtiers, arrived at Sadeq's house, and they were led to a banquet room specially decorated for their visit, with silk carpets and chandeliers and a dais for the Padishah to recline on. After the usual exchange of pleasantries, the royal guests were served the most varied and delicious meal they had ever had, accompanied by every fruit sherbet they could imagine and followed by a variety of sweets and ices. The meal over, they thanked Sadeq, praised the skill of his cook, and left.

The Padishah wondered how a young man like Sadeq could become rich enough to afford such a grand house and lavish banquet. In those days it took a man a lifetime to accumulate a fortune; it wasn't like today when some people seem to get rich in no time at all. As a result a *Haji* was always an old man. The King thought that Sadeq was bound to have a trade secret, some special ingredient or recipe that made his food so irresistible, and he wished to discover it. He summoned two of his most cunning spies and ordered them to find out the source of Sadeq's fortune; failing this they would be jailed for life.

The two men began to confer. They knew that Sadeq himself would never part with his secret, so they befriended his loyal assistant, a guileless youth called Hassan, and they managed to win his confidence. Hassan revealed to them that the food came from a little room behind the shop and that no one had ever been there except Sadeq himself. They cajoled and flattered and reasoned with Hassan, and eventually they persuaded him to let them into Sadeq's private back-room, saying that they meant no harm; they only wished to learn what secret ingredients he used to make his food so irresistibly appetizing. The naive Hassan believed them and one evening when his boss went out and left Hassan to lock up, he allowed the Shah's spies in.

Once inside the little room, the King's spies hid behind a curtain and waited. At noon Sadeq came in and closed the door. He then picked up an empty silver saucepan and a spoon from a cupboard, sat down and began to drum the saucepan murmuring, 'Saffron-rice with stew! Saffron-rice with stew!' The saucepan filled up with steaming hot food whose aroma made them giddy. What magic was this? They held their breath and waited. Sadeq sent out the food and repeated the formula, this time mentioning a different stew, and again the container filled up. He also tapped the crystal bowl and mentioned a variety of sherbets. This went on until every client was served and the last one had left. Then he tidied away his precious dishes, locked them up, said goodbye to Hassan and went home.

The spies were let out by their accomplice and went straight to the Palace to report to the Shah. Well, my dear, you know how greedy human beings can be — the more they have, the more they want. The Padishah was seized with envy at such a miraculous source of income and he wanted to own the magic items. If one simple young man could become so rich in such a short time, imagine what he could do! Instead of raising taxes and risking his subjects' displeasure, he could feed the entire population and make himself still more loved and honoured than he already was. He sent the spies back to fetch the silver saucepan and spoon, which they did by breaking into the shop at night.

The next day Sadeq arrived at his shop as usual and at noon he went into his back-room to produce the food for lunch, but — horror of horrors! — his saucepan, spoon and crystal bowl had gone! What could have happened to them? He called in Hassan and quizzed him, and Hassan eventually confessed that he had allowed his two friends to hide behind the curtain and learn the secret of his boss's trade.

Sadeq beat his head with both hands and howled, 'Ashes-on-my head![2] What have you done, you wretched fool? You have ruined us all!' Who were the two men and where could he find them, he asked. Hassan didn't have a clue. They had told him that they meant no harm and he had believed them.

While Sadeq and Hassan were arguing, a neighbour came in to announce that the King was giving a free lunch to the whole town. Sadeq immediately realized what had happened and who was now in possession of his precious silver saucepan, spoon and crystal bowl. He ran to the Royal Palace and saw that indeed the food being served had the inebriating aroma and mouth-watering taste of his own. He demanded to be let in to see the King and to be given back his saucepan and spoon. He made such a noise that the Grand Vizir was alerted and, seeing that the crowd was becoming curious and listening to Sadeq's accusations, he ordered his men to horse-whip him and throw him out at once, saying that if he persisted in making a row and disturbing the peace he would be hanged.

Beaten and bruised, Sadeq dragged himself back home and told his mother the whole story. She tried to console him, telling him to trust in Providence, but deep down she was as desperate as he was, remembering their past poverty to which they would now surely return.

After he had recovered from the shock, Sadeq ran to the well into which the crow had disappeared and sitting on the edge started crying and lamenting, 'Give me back my *donbeh* or my money! You merciless bird!'

Presently a hand emerged from the well holding a bridle, while a voice ordered, 'Take this from me.' As soon as Sadeq took the bridle the hand disappeared and a donkey rose from the well and stood beside him. It was richly harnessed and looked healthy and strong. Sadeq thought that at least he could sell it in the Bazaar for a good price and start a new business with the money.

As he was riding back to town he wanted to stop and pick an apple from a road-side tree, so he pulled the bridle and said, 'Whoa!', whereupon the donkey made a rude noise and three gold sovereigns dropped from his bottom. Sadeq picked up the coins, put them in his pocket and rode his donkey home, wondering what magic animal this was that produced gold sovereigns instead of manure. He went home and told his mother that the donkey was even more miraculous than his silver saucepan and spoon, and proceeded to demonstrate. 'Whoa!' he said, and again the donkey made a rude noise and dropped three gold sovereigns.

Soon Sadeq was rich again, but this time he kept his donkey hidden in a shed at the bottom of his garden where nobody could know of its existence, not even the contrite and loyal Hassan.

One day Sadeq wanted to go to the *Hammam* and, feeling tired, he decided to ride instead of walking as he usually did. He tied his donkey to a tree outside the *Hammam* and told the children who were playing in the street to keep an eye on it, adding, 'But whatever you do, never pull the bridle and say "Whoa!" to it, or it will kick you hard and break your shins.' He then went in, had a good bath, smoked a hubble-bubble and ate a sorbet in the resting-room, and emerged feeling refreshed.

Now, in his absence the inquisitive children played with the donkey, and at some point one of them pulled the bridle and said, 'Whoa!', whereupon the animal made a rude noise and dropped three gold sovereigns. The boys gathered the coins and ran to tell the bath-owner and his assistants, who took the magic donkey and tethered an identical one in its place.

Sadeq came out of the *Hammam*, found his donkey and rode it home. Just before locking it in the shed, he pulled the bridle and said, 'Whoa!' Instead of dropping the usual gold sovereigns, the donkey stood there, looking dumb.

Sadeq panicked, ran back to the baths and asked the children what they had done with his donkey in his absence. They denied any knowledge of the magical animal, but told him that the bath-owner had taken the donkey home and brought it back later. Hassan realized what had happened and went to the owner demanding the return of his donkey. The bath-owner and his assistant laughed at him, told him that he had evidently taken leave of his senses, gave him a thorough thrashing and kicked him out.

What could he do now? Once again he was the victim of his own naivety. In desperation he went back to the well and addressed the invisible crow. 'Give me back my *donbeh* or my money, you merciless bird!' he said, and wept with despair. Presently a hand appeared holding a box with a stick inside it and a voice came from the bottom of the well enjoining, 'Don't drum the box with the stick shouting "Hit-and-kill! Hit-and-kill!" unless you really mean it.'

Sadeq took the box and went home. Once in his room he closed the door, opened the box and with the stick struck it, saying, 'Hit-and-kill! Hit-and-kill!' Immediately three warriors in full battle dress, their swords drawn, stood before him and said, 'At your service, Sir! Who shall we hit? Who shall we kill?'

Sadeq was flabbergasted! What manner of prodigy was this? He told the soldiers to go back where they came from and wait for his next order, whereupon they shrivelled into dots and disappeared inside the box.

Sadeq hid his miraculous new possession in a cupboard and went straight to the Royal Palace. There he sent a message to the Padishah that he wanted his silver saucepan and spoon back within three days, and that otherwise he would declare war against him. The courtiers guffawed at his presumption, thinking he had gone completely out of his mind, but Sadeq did not react to their taunts and went home.

Three days later he returned, this time taking his box with him, and asked for his silver saucepan and crystal bowl. Again the Palace officials laughed at him.

'Very well then,' he said. 'If that is the King's reaction, it is war!'

He walked away to a field, took out his magic box and hit it with the stick shouting, 'Hit and kill! Hit and kill!'

Immediately three fully equipped soldiers appeared. 'We are at your command, Sir,' they said. 'Who shall we hit? Who shall we kill?'

He hit the box again and repeated the *vird* (magic formula), and presently another three well-equipped soldiers appeared. He went on many times until he had a large army and they marched to the Palace. A mighty battle ensued between the Palace Guards and Sadeq's army, which the latter won. Eventually the King capitulated and Sadeq's magic saucepan was given back to him. Sadeq marched his soldiers away and, once out of the Palace gates, he ordered them back into the box.

The next day he went to the *Hammam* and demanded his donkey back. The owner laughed at him and slapped his face, and when Sadeq persisted, he summoned some of his minions to come and give him a thorough beating. But Sadeq managed to escape and, once in the fields, he tapped his magic box saying, 'Hit and kill! Hit and kill!' Presently he had a dozen sturdy, armed soldiers, and they went back to the *Hammam*. A pitched battle ensued. Only when he was nearly annihilated did the wicked bath-owner accept defeat and give back Sadeq's donkey.

With his magic saucepan, donkey and box Sadeq became as rich and powerful as the Padishah himself. After all, he had all the food, all the gold and all the soldiers that he wanted. He built a huge palace and filled it with sumptuous carpets and furniture, and when it was ready he asked the Padishah to dinner again. This time the reception was even more lavish. After dinner Sadeq respectfully asked the Padishah for Princess Dorna's hand and was accepted with alacrity. After all, what better suitor could he find?

Theirs was the wedding of the century, with forty days of public festivity. The whole country rejoiced, and the couple lived happily ever after and had many children.

Haroon al-Rashid's Favourite Concubine

There was one and there was none/Except for God there was no one.

They say that when the great Caliph Haroon al-Rashid was at the height of his power and ruled over half the world, he had a Harem of four hundred wives and concubines. They lived in his palace in Baghdad, the capital of his empire. Every evening when the day's work was finished, he left the State Rooms and went to the Harem to see his women and spend the evening enjoying himself in their company. You can imagine how the women vied with each other to make themselves attractive to him, with pretty clothes and alluring make-up and delectable scents. Dinner was served and afterwards musicians played and dancers danced, while the Caliph cast his expert eyes around, now flirting with one, now caressing another of the women, and finally he took one of them by the hand and went off with her to his bed-chamber. All the others were left full of envy.

Among the hosts of servants and maids and slave-girls in the Harem there was an old woman called Zeinab, who was a beauty expert and knew all the secrets of the profession: how to use plants and roots and berries to concoct creams and lotions; how to devise make-up and coiffures for each woman to enhance her attractiveness. In her hands even the plainest girl became as lovely as the moon, let alone these *houris* who had been hand-picked for the Caliph among the empire's beauties or bought at the slave-markets of Zanzibar and Damascus.

Zeinab had a grandson called Akbar, who was the light of her eyes and the only joy of her life. His parents had died when he was a child and his grandmother had brought him up with care and devotion. She had apprenticed him to a butcher who had treated him kindly and trained him well. Now Akbar was twenty, handsome and well-mannered, and his old boss was so pleased with him that he left him in charge of his business when he went off on the pilgrimage to Mecca. Akbar's grandmother thanked God for his progress, and began looking around for a suitable wife for him.

The Harem was a closed, self-contained world, with a legion of eunuchs and slaves and servants who guarded the apartments and took care of the chores. From time to time one of Haroon's women was taken out in the Caliph's gilded coach for a tour of the city and perhaps to buy something that took her fancy; she would be accompanied by her favourite slave-girl and a watchful eunuch. People stopped to look at the beautiful carriage, but the women were hidden from view by curtains and no one could see their faces.

One day the coach stopped at a goldsmith's near Akbar's shop, and as Haroon's concubine was stepping down, he glimpsed her pale, slim ankle, adorned with a gold anklet This sight hit his heart like an arrow and he fell madly in love. The woman noticed the handsome young man standing in front of his shop, his face framed with a downy short beard, his dark eyes burning with passion, and she too felt a stab in her heart and a rush of feelings such as she had not known before. She spent a few minutes at the goldsmith's and left.

Try as he might, Akbar could not get her out of his mind. He lost his sleep and his appetite, and he grew pale and thin. Zeinab noticed the change in her beloved grandson and asked for an explanation. At first Akbar would not say anything, but one day he opened his heart and told his grandmother the truth: he was desperately in love, with no less a woman than one of Haroon's wives.

From the description of the anklet, Zeinab knew at once who the woman was. She hit her head with both hands as a sign of calamity and said, 'God help us! She is Amineh Khatoun, a new concubine and the Caliph's current favourite! You can sooner have the stars in Heaven than her! There are plenty of beautiful girls in our town, and you can choose any one of them: why ask for the impossible?'

But Akbar was adamant: either he would have the woman who had captured his heart or he would pine to death. His old grandmother pondered the hopeless situation for a while and finally said, 'I'll see what I can do, but you must follow my instructions exactly and without questioning.' Akbar promised he would.

She told him that since no male entered the Harem except Haroon himself, the only way for Akbar to gain access was to disguise himself to look exactly like the Caliph and pretend to be him. To achieve the likeness, the first thing Akbar had to do was to let his beard grow longer and gain a little weight. Next he had to dress like the Caliph and learn to behave like him. Having been their beauty counsellor for so long, Zeinab had the confidence of the Harem women, and from one of them she obtained a set of Haroon's clothes and sandals, together with a bag of gold coins and *noql* (sweetmeat made with slivers of almond covered with sugar) which he usually kept in his pockets to distribute when necessary.

Dressed in Haroon's regal clothes, with his shiny black beard and healthy complexion, Akbar looked the image of the Caliph, and Zeinab made him rehearse Haroon's manners and behaviour in the Harem until she was sure that he was ready. Now all they needed was an opportunity. It soon came, when one evening Haroon told his Harem that he would be away hunting gazelles in the desert and would not be visiting them for a couple of nights. The next evening at sunset Zeinab took Akbar to the Palace, let him in through a secret door, and told him to go in and pretend to be Haroon, saying he had decided to postpone his hunting expedition.

Meanwhile Amineh Khatoun was also love-sick, but there was nothing she could do — she was a bird in a cage; in a few months Haroon would get tired of her and she would be like all his other women in the Harem, her youth withering away, her life wasted. She sighed and became listless, and no one knew what was the matter with her and why, instead of rejoicing at her good fortune, she was unhappy.

Anyway, Akbar went inside the Harem and as if to the manner born, acted exactly like the Caliph, following his grandmother's instructions. First he walked confidently along a long corridor between two lines of eunuchs, who bowed down as he passed. At the end was a set of steps leading to a huge door. He knocked three times; the door was opened by invisible hands and he entered another corridor. He walked on until he reached a large hall where he found a bell, which he shook vigorously, as his grandmother had instructed.

Presently a bevy of ravishing women rushed forward to greet him, saying how glad they were he had changed his mind and not gone hunting. He caressed the hair of one and patted the cheek of another while looking around the room for the one he wanted.

At the back stood a very beautiful and aloof young woman looking at him, with ardent black eyes and a mysterious smile on her lips, as if sharing a secret joke with him. He found her so desirable that he forgot to look for the anklet, and motioned to her to come forward. He scattered the gold coins and *noql* among the others like confetti and, while they were busy picking them up, he led his companion of the night to the bed-chamber and closed the door. Only when he took her in his arms and began to caress her did he notice the anklet: it was the one he had glimpsed all those months ago, and she was indeed Amineh Khatoun, the woman he had longed for ever since.

She of course had recognized him at once, despite his disguise, and had been smiling with amusement. She was coquettish, now pushing him away and laughing, now beckoning him back, teasing and asking for favours before she bestowed hers.

'How young you have become since your last visit!' she said, smiling. 'Have you been given the elixir of youth? How soft and shiny your beard has become', and so on.

Akbar enjoyed her banter, and he took a seal from the bedside table and used it to give her a district of Baghdad as a token of his special affection for her. 'Which quarter would you like?' he asked her, and she chose the area where Akbar's shop was.

Now hear about the real Haroon al-Rashid. At the last minute he cancelled the hunting expedition on the advice of his astrologers and went instead to the Harem as usual.

When he entered, the eunuchs were puzzled. 'What mystery is this?' they said. 'He came through an hour ago. This has never happened before: how did he go out and come back in again without us seeing him? Something must be afoot.'

Haroon reached the hall and rang the bell, and the women rushed forward to greet him, wondering why he had left his bed-chamber so soon and what had happened to Amineh Khatoun whom he had whisked away only an hour or so ago. Not seeing his favourite among them, Haroon asked where she was, and when they pointed to his bed-chamber he dismissed them all and hurried to find her, delighted that she had anticipated his desire and gone in to prepare herself. But as he entered the chamber he was stopped by a most extraordinary sight: his favourite concubine was in the arms of a man who looked exactly like himself.

'Who are you?' he exclaimed, wondering whether he was hallucinating or if a jinn was playing a trick on him.

'I am the great Haroon al-Rashid, the Commander of the Faithful,' Akbar replied.

Reassured that Akbar was a real person and not a jinn, Haroon became furious and shouted at him, 'How dare you presume? I am the Caliph, and I will have you drawn and quartered at once!'

Akbar remained unperturbed. 'I am the Caliph,' he said, 'and I can have you beheaded immediately for entering my apartments and pretending to be me.'

A heated argument ensued, each insisting that he was the real Caliph. Finally Haroon called in the eunuchs and asked them, 'Which of us is the real Haroon al-Rashid?' Half of them chose Akbar and half Haroon. In desperation Haroon called in his wives and concubines and asked them the same question. Again one half chose Akbar and the other Haroon.

At this point Haroon lost his temper and attacked his rival, but Akbar was younger and more vigorous, and he overcame the Caliph quickly, knocked him to the ground and sat on his chest.

Haroon realized he was defeated, and that Akbar could cut his throat and take his place. So he begged him to spare his life. Akbar had no ambition to be the Caliph and have the responsibility of running an empire, and he said, 'I will spare your life if you promise to spare mine.' Haroon swore on the Holy Quran that he would not punish him.

When they both stood up, Haroon asked Akbar what was his purpose in impersonating him and what he really wanted. Akbar told him the whole story, adding that he was content being a butcher and that his only ambition in life was to marry Amineh Khatoun, live with her and love her for the rest of his life.

'Oh Commander of the Faithful!' he pleaded. 'You can have all the beautiful women in the world. In a few months you will get tired of Amineh Khatoun and choose another, while I shall love her forever and will never look at another woman.'

Haroon al-Rashid was moved by Akbar's sincerity and ardour, and he agreed to let him have his favourite concubine, thinking that, after all, he was beginning to tire of her. He told Akbar that because he had risked his life for love, with courage and ingenuity, he would grant his wish and reward him with a suitable dowry for his bride. Saying this he picked up the Royal Seal and prepared to sign the deed for a whole district of the city.

'Which part of my capital do you like best?' he asked the couple, and they chose the area around Akbar's shop. 'But we already have it,' they said, and showed him the deed Akbar had already signed and sealed. Haroon endorsed it and handed it to them, with his blessings.

Akbar was now a very rich man, and when his boss came back from pilgrimage, he handed over the shop to him and went to live with his bride and his old mother in a grand house nearby, vowing to devote his time to good works. He and Amineh Khatoun lived happily ever after and had several children. As for Zeinab, she had a comfortable old age, and gave her services free to whoever consulted her. She it was who coined the saying 'Where there is love, there is a way.'

The Secret of Laughter

There was one and there was none/Except for God there was no one.

Once upon a time in the country of India there was a widow who had a son called Shoja ('Brave'), and they lived in a modest hut on the edge of a small, far-away town near the forest. She was poor and unlettered, had no money and no possessions, but she was proud and hard-working, and she was sure that once her son grew up he would learn a trade, earn a decent living and make their life easier. She took any jobs she could find, however menial, with good humour and dignity, so she could raise her son; she sent him to the village *maktab* (primary school) to learn reading and writing and then to the saddler as an apprentice to learn a secure profession.

In this way they managed to survive until Shoja grew up into a handsome and pleasant young man. Like his mother he was energetic and self-possessed, and he did not lack ambition. At work he was eager and diligent, quick to pick up all the subtleties of the saddler's trade, and his boss was very pleased with him. At eighteen he was admired by the whole town; mothers wanted him for their daughters and began dropping hints to the widow. In those days marriages were arranged between families; it was not like today when parents are lucky if they are invited to the wedding.

One day Shoja's boss gave him some saddles he had made for the King, and asked him to travel to the city and deliver them to the Palace. Shoja was grateful for this mark of confidence and excited at the prospect of seeing a big town for the first time. Early the next morning he set off, in the company of other travellers and hawkers, and they arrived at the city gates by nightfall.

He put up at the *caravanserai*, and the next day he went to the King's Palace to deliver the goods. He was led to a small reception room and asked to wait for the Chamberlain.

Presently he heard the sound of voices and laughter outside, and looking through the windows he saw a bevy of young girls playing in the garden. Each more beautiful than the next, and all of them with flowing hair and fine clothes of many colours, they looked like fairies in an enchanted domain. One in particular caught his eye: even more vivacious and ravishing than the rest, she was clearly leading their games. Surely she was Princess Shahla, the King's only daughter, whose sixteenth birthday had recently been celebrated throughout the realm and whom her father loved more than anyone in the world. Shoja was lost in the contemplation of her beauty when the Chamberlain came in. He took the saddles, paid for them and accompanied Shoja to the door, with greetings and compliments for his boss.

All through the journey back Shoja could not get Princess Shahla out of his mind. He was so smitten with her that he forgot about the difference in their stations: he a poor saddler's apprentice, she the King's only daughter, the gap between them as wide as an ocean. When he arrived home he said nothing to his mother, but he lost his good cheer and became quiet and pensive. His mother noticed the change in his mood and worried, but she held her tongue until one day Shoja volunteered to talk.

'Dear mother,' he said, 'you have been urging me to think about getting married. Well, I have found the girl of my dreams, and I want you to go and ask for her hand.

'God be praised!' said the widow. 'Who is she?'

'Princess Shahla, the King's daughter,' he replied.

His mother thought he was joking, but soon realized he was serious, and she said, 'What witches' brew did they give you in the city? What will become of us if you have lost your mind?'

Shoja assured her that he was perfectly sane, and told her to go to the Palace and simply ask the King for his daughter's hand, as custom required. Seeing that she could not make him see reason, she gave in. She borrowed some suitable clothes from her neighbours, got herself up to look as smart as she could, and went off to town. She asked the way to the King's Palace and then sweet-talked the guards and servants to let her in.

As luck would have it, this was the day the King was holding a public audience in the throne-room and receiving petitioners. When it was her turn, Shoja's mother stepped forward, bowed deeply and said, 'Your Majesty, I have come to beg for Princess Shahla's hand for my son Shoja. He is eighteen, healthy and honest, a skilful saddler, and he will be as good, gentle and loving a husband to your beautiful daughter as he has been a dutiful son to me.'

So stunned were the King and his courtiers by this presumptuous speech that for a moment no one said anything, waiting for the King to say, 'Off with her head!' Instead, to everyone's astonishment, he calmly said, 'Very well, tell your son to find the secret of laughter and bring it to me. If he makes me laugh, he shall have my daughter, but should he come to my presence, try to make me laugh and fail, he will be beheaded instantly.'

Now this King was a just and benevolent ruler and he had made his country prosperous and his people content, but ever since his Queen's death in childbirth a decade before our story began, he had suffered from melancholia; as a result a dark cloud hung over his Court and everyone was afraid of him. His courtiers tried everything to amuse him and make him more cheerful, but nothing ever worked. The cleverest comedians, magicians and conjurers in the world were summoned to his Palace and performed for him, but the King's lips never parted with a smile of amusement, nor did the laughter of surprise and admiration ever light up his grim face. Those who had known him for a long time had forgotten the sound of his laughter and his Palace had the silence of the tomb. As a result his gloom infected his whole kingdom and his people lived in fear of his anger, for his mood impaired his judgement and sometimes he was unduly harsh in the punishment he meted out to wrongdoers. So when he told Shoja to make him laugh or else die in the attempt, no one believed the young man would even try.

But Shoja accepted the challenge. 'I will find the secret of laughter and cure the King's melancholia,' he said when his mother gave him the King's message.

Now there was a famous sorcerer whom no one had ever seen but whose reputation had spread all over the country. They said he was the Abu Ali Sina (Avicenna) of the day, that he knew the properties of plants and the language of animals and could perform miracles no one had ever witnessed before. He even knew the alchemical formula to turn base metal into gold.

'Surely he must know the secret of laughter,' said Shoja. 'I will find him and learn it from him.'

His mother tried to dissuade him, wondering whether this sorcerer really existed, since no one had ever seen him and those who had gone in search of him had never come back. Perhaps he was only a figment of people's imagination? Or some evil demon in the desert who trapped travellers with false promises? But Shoja was determined to try and find him. He asked permission from his boss for a long leave of absence, which the saddler granted, as the pursuit of knowledge is the noblest endeavour, and he told Shoja that he would be welcome back whenever he returned. So one fine morning Shoja left the village at the crack of dawn and set off to discover the secret of laughter.

He walked and walked, through villages and forests and hilly lands, until he reached a wilderness with no sign of life. He felt hungry and tired, but he went on until he reached a tiny oasis, with a single tree and a small pool. He sat down in the shade of the tree, ate some of the bread and cheese his mother had packed for him, and was so overcome by fatigue that he fell fast asleep.

Presently he was discovered by a young girl who was walking by the pool. She was surprised by his presence, as few travellers went through this barren and isolated part of the country, and she tiptoed up to look at him. Shoja's face was so beautiful and his expression so innocent that she fell in love with him there and then.

She waited for him to wake up and when he did, she told him that her name was Zara and that she lived with her father nearby. She asked what brought him to that God-forsaken part of the world. Shoja told her his story from beginning to end, and what he was looking for. Zara was so touched by his honesty and trust that, in spite of her own feelings for him, she decided as best she could to help him gain what he wished.

She told him that her father was the man Shoja was looking for, the greatest sorcerer that had ever lived, that not even Abu Ali Sina could rival his knowledge and power, and that no one else could help him find the secret of laughter and cure the King's melancholia. Unfortunately he was a mean man, jealous of his powers and ruthless with anyone who tried to emulate him. He snared those who came near him by promising to teach them al-chemy and magic, made them work hard on his land and killed them as soon as they learnt something of his skills.

'You are not the first young man who has come here in search of magical knowledge,' she said to Shoja. 'Dozens have been over the years and all have perished by his hand.' Saying this she pointed to a pile of bones and skulls behind a big rock and added, 'That is what remains of all the young men who have been here before you.'

When Shoja heard this, instead of borrowing two extra legs to add to his own and run away like the wind, he told her he still wanted to try.

'In that case you must do exactly as I tell you,' said Zara. 'You must observe carefully everything my father does and memorize every *vird* he utters, but pretend not to see or understand anything. When he quizzes you, give silly answers which have nothing to do with his questions, and if he demands that you repeat one of his experiments, bungle it, so that it doesn't work. After a while he will think you're an idiot and he'll let you go. But be careful! One word or action that indicates you've learnt something, and you're done for. You'll be killed on the spot like all the others before you.' Zara told him how she and her mother had pleaded with her father to spare the lives of the young apprentices, but in vain. Her mother had died recently, unable to bear her husband's wickedness any longer, and she was the only person left in the world whom the Sorcerer treated with kindness.

As they were talking, the Sorcerer appeared and asked who the young man was, and Shoja told him that he wanted to be his apprentice. 'Do you now?' he said. 'Very well, you stay with me for a few months and we shall see if you have any talent.'

They walked for a while until they reached the Sorcerer's house. He uttered a *vird*, the door opened as if by invisible hands, and they went in. The Sorcerer showed Shoja his room, saying, 'This is where your predecessors have lived', and Shoja's heart sank at the thought of all those bones.

The next day the Sorcerer told Shoja to go with him and learn to shepherd his flock of sheep on the mountainside. After a couple of hours Shoja saw that the sheep were suddenly changed into a herd of cattle. Flabbergasted, he said nothing, pretending not to notice anything, and continued to watch over the animals. By late afternoon they had changed into horses, and on the return journey home at sundown they had become a flock of sheep again.

In the following days the Sorcerer performed the same sort of tricks: the sheep turned into a flight of geese, a pond-full of fish, and back again to sheep. He could change anything whatever to anything he wanted. At night the house became a castle lit with a thousand candles, in daytime it was a poor man's cottage covered in cobwebs; one minute they were eating a superb meal from golden plates, the next a piece of dry bread from a tin bowl.

Still Shoja said nothing and expressed no surprise. He behaved for all the world as if he had always lived in such circumstances and witnessed such wonders. But he observed every gesture and memorized every *vird* that brought about the extraordinary transformations he witnessed.

The Sorcerer was puzzled: what manner of a young man was this, he wondered. All the others were keen to learn and show off how well they could perform, while this one seemed always in a dream. After a while he began to test him, but Shoja gave him stupid answers, such as 'The sky is blue', or 'Water has no colour', or something totally unconnected to his questions. And when he asked Shoja to perform conjuring tricks, he always bungled them.

After six months he said to his daughter, 'This boy is too stupid to learn anything' and he threw Shoja out. In a flash the house disappeared and all around was nothing but empty wilderness.

Shoja walked on and reached the oasis where he had fallen asleep when he first arrived. There he found Zara waiting for him. She was very sad to see him go, but he promised her that if he succeeded in marrying the King's daughter he would send for her and release her from her bondage, and she would become his wife's *mounis* (lady-in-waiting) and his own sister. And so the two friends parted with expressions of gratitude from Shoja and of hope and trust from Zara.

Back at home Shoja's mother was overjoyed to see him safe and sound, and the two spent the evening talking about his adventures and his plans, but he didn't tell her anything about the Sorcerer and the knowledge of magic he had acquired.

The next day Shoja told his mother that there was a horse tied to the knocker of their front door. She should take it to the animal fair in town and sell it for a hundred *dirhams* — for it was a magnificent specimen — but she must keep the bridle: 'Don't forget, no matter how much money you are offered you must not part with the bridle.'

The mother agreed and went out to find the horse. At that moment Shoja changed himself into a lovely chestnut stallion, tethered to the doorknob. His mother rode it to the Bazaar where the fair took place every month and had no trouble selling it for two hundred *dirhams*. She went home full of excitement and hung the bridle on a hook. Shoja, who had changed himself into the bridle when the horse was sold, turned back into himself as soon as his mother went out of the room, and with the money they bought food and clothes and improved their derelict home.

Next Shoja turned himself into a bull, which his mother took to the cattle market and sold to the highest bidder. This time his instructions were: 'Sell the animal but keep the rope that is round his neck', which she did.

And so every month Shoja changed into a different animal — a camel, a milk cow, a flock of geese — which his mother took to the market and sold at a good price. Gradually they became rich and the mother almost forgot the hardships of the past. Shoja thought that, if the sorcery he had learnt could not amuse the King and make him laugh, perhaps he could make himself rich enough to become an acceptable suitor for his daughter.

Meanwhile the Sorcerer heard that there was an old woman who appeared at the horse and cattle market every month with the best animals anyone had ever seen, even better than his own, and sold them for a great deal of money. He became suspicious and wondered who she was and where she had got them from. Could it be that he had a rival? He suddenly remembered Shoja, the only young man who had got away from him, and he began to worry.

For his part Shoja felt that his master had heard of his exploits — sorcerers can read each other's minds — and next time his mother was going to the market with a black mare to sell, he told her that there would be a man at the fair, full of charm and courtesy, who would try and buy the horse from her.

'Sell him the horse,' he said. 'But on no account must you part with the bridle, otherwise you'll never see me again.' His mother promised.

At the fair Shoja spotted the old Sorcerer in the crowd. For his part the Sorcerer immediately recognized Shoja and, boiling with anger, he bid for the horse and bought it at four times the expected price. Shoja's mother handed him the horse and kept the bridle, but he protested, saying that the price included the bridle. An argument ensued, the mother refusing to sell, the wicked Sorcerer offering more and more money, and even a gold-trimmed bridle in its place.

As it happened the *Qazi* was passing by, heard the argument and decreed that the bridle should be given to the buyer. For her part Shoja's mother, overcome by the man's insistence and thinking that her son would not mind — after all what was so special about an ordinary bridle compared to the one she was taking home? — accepted, and handed the old bridle to the horse's new owner. She didn't notice that the horse looked at her piteously, tears running down its face.

The Sorcerer mounted the mare and as soon as he left the fair, he guffawed and gave it a hard kick, saying, 'Now I've got you! You thought you were clever. You tricked me into letting you go. Now we shall see who's the cleverer!'

He kicked and whipped the mount mercilessly until they reached the oasis where Shoja had first met Zara. There she was again, sitting in the shade of the tree. She immediately recognized Shoja as the horse and her heart sank with pity.

Her father told her to go and fetch his big slaughtering knife and bring it to him, for he wished to dispatch the mare forthwith.

Zara went and hid the knife somewhere safe and came back saying, 'I cannot find it; it has vanished.'

So he sent her to get his sword and again she came back empty-handed. It was the same with his dagger and cutlass, until he got angry with her and shouted, 'Hold on to this accursed horse and I will go and find a knife myself.'

As soon as the Sorcerer let go of the bridle, Shoja turned himself into a fox and dashed away and hid in the bushes. When the Sorcerer came back with a big knife, the mare had vanished.

'What happened? Where is he?' he asked his daughter, ready to cut her throat if she lied, but she told him the truth, saying Shoja had changed into a fox and bounded off.

Immediately the Sorcerer turned himself into a hound and ran after the fox, but just as he was about to catch him, the fox became a pigeon and flew into the sky. In a second the hound became a hawk; he chased the bird in the cloudless sky and opened his talons to snatch it.

Just then Shoja noticed he was flying over the roof of the King's Palace and the image of his beloved Princess Shahla came to his eyes. His heart filled with longing and, forgetting the danger of the hawk, he alighted on the chimney stack to look at the garden: perhaps he could catch a glimpse of her! In those days houses had an opening in the roof which allowed the air to circulate and cool the room below when the weather was hot.[1] As the hawk dived down to dig his talons into the pigeon, Shoja changed himself into a pomegranate and fell through the air shaft below.

As it happened the King was sitting there, smoking a *nargileh* and talking to his Vizir and counsellors, and the pomegranate fell into his lap. He was amazed. 'What miracle is this?' he wondered aloud. 'This is not the season for pomegranates. How could such a large, red fruit come down from the roof?'

At that moment the hawk changed into a wandering dervish and knocked on the door, begging to be given some sustenance. He was invited in and given food and beverage, but he rejected everything: the only thing he wanted was the pomegranate His Majesty had on his lap.

The King refused to part with the fruit, saying that it was a sign from Heaven, a gift of God, arriving out of season and out of the blue: he was going to keep it.

The obstinate dervish insisted and begged and cried, pretending that he had a peculiar ailment for which the only cure was pomegranate. Eventually the King got so angry at his impertinence that he threw the pomegranate at him. It fell on the ground and burst open, and the grains scattered all over the place, whereupon the dervish turned into a chicken and began to gobble them up as fast as he could. In no time he had swallowed the lot, except for one single grain that had rolled to the King's foot. It was Shoja, who quickly turned himself into a fox again, pounced on the chicken and bit its head off.

Observing all this, the King burst out laughing. The Vizir and counsellors were so delighted that they began to laugh too. So did the servants and the guards, and presently the whole assembly was laughing aloud. For the first time since the Queen's death the sound of laughter resounded through the Palace.

Amid the general mirth the fox turned himself into a handsome young man. It was none other than Princess Shahla's devoted suitor. He prostrated himself before the King and reminded him of his promise: that if he found the secret of laughter, he would give him his daughter in marriage. Shoja then told the story of his adventures and the King was so impressed with his courage and devotion that he took his hand and sat him down beside his throne. He then summoned his daughter, Princess Shahla, and said to her, 'Here at last is a man worthy of you.'

Shoja and Shahla were married amid public jubilation, but Shoja did not forget his promise to Zara: he invited her to the wedding and received her as an honoured guest. She became the Princess's companion, married the Vizir's son, and they all lived happily ever after.

The King and the Prophet Khizr

There was one and there was none/Except for God there was no one.

There was once a king called Jahangir who ruled over a large country in Hindustan. He was his father's only son and only eighteen years old when the old King died, leaving him in charge of a prosperous realm and contented people. Soon after this, Jahangir married Shahpasand, a beautiful princess from a neighbouring kingdom, and settled down to govern his country. He had three elderly viziers, chosen by his father from among hundreds of courtiers in the hope that they would counsel the young King judiciously and protect him from rivals, hypocrites and ambitious neighbours. To them Jahangir added a fourth vizir, younger and nearer to his own age.

Time passed. The young King was popular and at peace with his neighbours; the treasury was full, the harvests abundant and people said that young Jahangir was indeed a blessing on the nation.

There was only one dark cloud in the otherwise unblemished sky of his life: he had no children. He loved his wife tenderly with all his heart and the two of them tried every remedy: doctors and

gurus came from all over Hindustan and Farangistan and prescribed prayers and potions, while midwives and wise crones gave
the Queen old recipes and advice, but it was all to no avail.

In desperation the Queen suggested to her husband that he
take other wives and concubines; perhaps one of them would be
lucky enough to conceive and produce an heir. Reluctantly he
agreed, but still nothing happened — the women remained barren.

There was only one last hope: the intervention of the Prophet
Khizr, who lived in the Occult World from the beginning to the
end of time, and who once in a while, very rarely, appeared somewhere in the world, performed an astonishing miracle and vanished
again.

In those days important news and decrees were announced by
town criers, men with strong voices who stood in the middle of
public squares in towns and villages, beat their drums to attract
attention, and when a crowd had gathered, made the announce-
ment. In no time the news would spread and the whole population
would hear about it. So, on the advice of his viziers, the King sent
his criers all over the kingdom to proclaim that whosoever found
the Prophet Khizr and brought him to the Royal Court would
receive a reward of one thousand gold sovereigns.

This was a vast fortune, like a million today, and very tempt-
ing, but how could Khizr be found? It was an impossible task, since
he lived in the timeless Invisible World and materialized only when
and where he pleased. No one ever recognized him while he was
visible; only when he had disappeared, when it was too late to try
and keep him back, did people realize who he was. So when the
King's criers offered this huge prize for finding Khizr, nobody
came forward.

Now there was a cameleer who lived with his wife in a derelict
cottage on the edge of his village. He was called Ali-Asghar, and he
was very poor, owning nothing in the world but one single camel.

The animal was patient and hardy; he worked all day transporting heavy loads of goods to surrounding villages and towns, and he provided his owner with a meagre living. At night he was put in his shed with a sack of hay, and he seemed content with his lot.

Human beings are different from animals, for God has given them something called *Aql* — Reason — and so they ask questions. They worry about the future, and want something more than a piece of bread at the end of the day's work. Ali-Asghar complained to his wife, saying that he was getting old and tired, that sooner or later his camel would die, and then what would become of them?

'God will provide,' his gentle wife would say, trying to soothe him. She spent all day spinning wool and cotton for the farmers in the neighbourhood to earn a little more money, but still life was hard and her husband's brow was often furrowed with care.

One day at dawn when Ali-Asghar went to the shed to take his camel out and go to work, he discovered that his faithful animal had given up the ghost. What a catastrophe! He hit his head with both hands, moaning 'Ashes-on-my-head!', and cried out to his wife, who rushed in. When she saw the lifeless animal, she was equally devastated by the calamity. The camel was their livelihood; they had hoped that he would live several years more, perhaps even outlive them, and now he had gone.

The old man had no choice but to become a *khar-kan* — a thorn-seller. Every day he went to the nearby wilderness which was covered with thorn bushes and dug and collected a large load of thorn, which he then tied together with a rope and carried on his back to sell in the village. The villagers used thorn as firewood, especially to heat the water at the *Hammam*. The *khar-kan*'s work was hard, especially for a man getting on in years, but what else could he do?

It was at this time that he heard the King was offering one thousand gold sovereigns to whoever found Khizr and brought him to the Palace, and he decided to try his luck. His wife made every effort to dissuade him, saying that no one could find Khizr, since he lived in the Occult World and only appeared when he wished, but her husband was adamant: it was time to throw caution to the wind, for anything was better than their present life of want and worry.

So he went to the King's Palace and offered his services, on condition that he be paid the reward in advance, as he had to give up work and search all over the country for his quarry.

The King was doubtful: how could he trust an unknown *kharkan*? How could he be sure that this man would actually bring back the miracle-performing Khizr? But he was desperate, this was his last chance, and he agreed to pay on condition that if Ali-Asghar did not bring Khizr within forty days, he would pay back the gold or be put to death. The old cameleer accepted.

He returned home full of joy, showed the bag of gold to his wife and said that their tribulations were over, at least for now. Women are more down-to-earth than men, and Ali-Asghar's wife was apprehensive — what would they do after forty days? — but her husband reassured her. 'God is Great,' he said. He would find a solution for them. If not, Ali-Asghar would be beheaded, but he was getting old and it was better to live forty days in ease and abundance than forty years as a beast of burden.

The very next day Ali-Asghar began to spend the money. He had their crumbling cottage repaired and turned into a proper house, which he furnished with beautiful carpets and lamps and ornaments, and he filled their larder with provisions — sacks of flour and rice and pulses, tea and sugar, crates of vegetable and fruit, and all manner of spices and condiments — enough for a regiment. For the first time in their lives they could have any dish they fancied and as many meals as they wished.

Well, when people become rich, they quickly forget how poor they once were — as they say, 'A full belly can't remember being empty' — but Ali-Asghar and his wife did not forget. They paid their tithe and gave generously to the poor; they fed and clothed the needy around them, and once a week they offered a public dinner to which everybody was invited. People flocked from all over the district, ate as much as they could and filled their bowls with rice and stew to take home for the next day.

It was not long before Ali-Asghar's bag of gold sovereigns began to empty and the deadline of forty days was rapidly approaching. Ali-Asghar became more and more agitated; he had decided to live like a prince for forty days and die, but now that he had tasted a life of ease he had no wish to leave this world. All living creatures are afraid of death, but only human beings think about it in advance and fear it long before it comes, and Ali-Asghar could imagine his own end vividly. He even began to regret his foolish decision; perhaps he should have listened to his wife and been content with their lot. But what is done cannot be undone; he kept his worries to himself.

On the thirty-ninth day he and his wife spent their last gold sovereign on a lavish public dinner. The poor of the district ate the succulent food, washed it down with cool sherbets and prayed for Ali-Asghar's continuing health and prosperity and munificence, not knowing this was the last time they would see him. It was nearly midnight before the crowd left.

'In a few hours the dawn will break and the King's men will come to get me!' Ali-Asghar told his wife. 'What will become of you after I'm gone?' And they hugged and cried.

Presently there was a gentle knock on the door. Who could it be at that ungodly hour? Should they open up? Could it be one of the dinner guests who had left something behind? Or a traveller who had lost his way?

Finally they opened the door, and found an old wandering dervish, who asked for some water and if possible some food, as he had been on the road for days and his *kashkoul* (dervish's bowl)[1] was empty. They invited him in and Ali-Asghar's wife brought him the leftovers from the night's feast, which the Dervish ate with appetite. He then asked for shelter, saying that it was a dark, moonless night, that he might get lost, or be attacked by robbers or wild beasts, and that he would be grateful if they allowed him to spend the night there and leave at dawn. Naturally they accepted and offered him some bedding, but the Dervish said he did not need any, and he lay down, pulled his cloak over his head and was soon fast asleep.

His hosts, alas, could not do the same; they sat up all night waiting, hoping against hope that the King had forgotten about the gold. But no sooner had the first rays of the sun appeared on the horizon than they heard the clatter of horses' hooves outside and presently there was a knock, loud and urgent.

'Open up! We are the King's men,' shouted a voice.

When Ali-Asghar opened the door the men poured in and said they had been ordered to take him to the King's Court.

Meanwhile the Wandering Dervish woke up and saw everything: Ali-Asghar shaking with fear, his wife distraught and the King's men evidently ready to be rough if they encountered any resistance. He said to his host, 'I'll come with you; I have something to tell the King.'

The men agreed to let him accompany them: after all he was a dervish, a holy man who was no threat to anybody.

Once inside the Palace the cameleer and the old Wandering Dervish were ushered into the King's reception room, where he was sitting on his dais flanked by his viziers, two on either side, and surrounded by his inner circle of courtiers.

Addressing Ali-Asghar the King said, 'So, have you found the Prophet Khizr?'

Ali-Asghar replied that alas he had not, and all his efforts had proved fruitless.

'In that case you must give back the thousand gold sovereigns you were paid,' said the King, and Ali-Asghar had to admit that he had spent it all, to the last penny. The King reminded Ali-Asghar that he had demanded to be paid in advance, knowing that if he did not find Khizr within forty days and could not return the reward, his punishment would be death.

Ali-Asghar bowed his head and agreed. 'Yes, Your Majesty, I know, and I am at your mercy.'

The King was perplexed. He turned to his First Vizir and asked him what manner of death such a man deserved.

'If I were Your Majesty,' replied the First Vizir, 'I would cut him into four pieces and hang them at the four gates of the city as an example to the population.'

Hearing this, the Dervish, who was standing quietly at the back, said, 'It depends on the origin.' It seemed a non-sequitur from an old fool, and no one paid any attention.

The King then turned to his Second Vizir and asked, 'Tell me, in your view what manner of death does this man deserve?'

Quick as a flash, the Second Vizir replied, 'If I were Your Majesty I would throw him into the furnace of the *Hammam*, so that he would burn alive and discourage your subjects from any future fraud.'

Again the Dervish said, 'It depends on the origin.'

This time the King turned to his Third Vizir and asked the same question as to how the man should be punished. The Third Vizir's reply was: 'If I were Your Majesty I would pierce his body with the big needle they use to sew saddle bags, so that he bleeds to death painfully, as a warning to all miscreants.'

Once more the Dervish uttered, this time louder, 'It depends on the origin.' Again nobody took any notice of him.

Finally the King asked his Fourth Vizir, the young man he had chosen himself, what he should do with Ali-Asghar, and he replied, 'Your Majesty, you are the Sovereign, God's shadow on earth, the custodian of your people, you can do anything you wish. But whatever you do to this man, whether you behead him, quarter him, burn him or cut him to pieces, you will neither recover the gold nor see the Prophet Khizr. But if you pardon him, you will enjoy the pleasure of forgiveness and magnanimity, and receive God's blessing for your compassion and mercy. He is a poor thorn-seller and he was tempted by the offer of your reward. If I were Your Majesty I would forgive him and even give him a pension so that he can live out his old age in dignity. You will have his eternal gratitude and his prayers.'

At this the Dervish stepped forward and said, 'It depends on the origin', with a mysterious smile on his face.

The King became pensive, pondering the responses of his four vizirs. Three of them had advised the harshest punishments to make an example of the thorn-seller; the fourth had suggested total pardon. Meanwhile the audience waited with bated breath, eyes fixed on the royal countenance for any sign of his decision, while Ali-Asghar trembled in anticipation of torture and death.

Suddenly the King called out to the Dervish to come forward and explain what he had meant by muttering 'It depends on the origin' after each vizir had given his opinion. The Dervish was glad to comply, provided the King promised not to punish him whatever he said. The King agreed.

'Well, Sire,' the Dervish began, 'the First Vizir who suggested that you cut this old man into four pieces and hang them at the four gates of the city is the son of a butcher. He has witnessed his father slaughter innocent lambs, quarter them and hang them on hooks in his shop each day, and so he suggested that you do the same to this poor thorn-seller; his answer depends on his origin. The Second Vizir is the son of a public baths' attendant. He remembered his father shovelling coal into the furnace of the *Hammam* every day and he thought that the right punishment for wrong-doers was to burn them. The father of the Third Vizir was a saddle-bag maker and he recalled watching him sew pieces of rough cloth with big needles; so he suggested this man be pierced to pieces. As for the Fourth Vizir, he is the son of a noble prince. He watched his father dispense justice with mercy and he learnt from him how to be compassionate and forgiving. So you see, each man acted according to his origin, and that is what I meant when I said "It depends on the origin." Now it is up to Your Majesty to choose whose advice to follow.' Having finished, the Dervish stepped back and waited for the royal decision.

Before he pronounced his verdict the King wished to know how the Dervish had found out about his vizirs' background, since this was a well-kept secret: this was thought best so that they should be known only for their wisdom and sound judgement.

'Tell me, Dervish, who are you?' he asked. 'And how did you find out about my vizirs' origins?'

At that moment, instead of answering the King's questions, the Dervish simply vanished. Suddenly the spot where he had stood was empty. The audience gasped in wonder. 'God be praised!' they said, realizing that the old Dervish was none other than Khizr himself. But nobody was more flabbergasted than Ali-Asghar, and when the King asked him where he had found Khizr, he told him his story from beginning to the end.

For having found Khizr the King ordered that the blessed cameleer be given another thousand gold sovereigns and a monthly pension for the rest of his life. Soon the news of Khizr's appearance at the Royal Palace spread everywhere and the whole population rejoiced, expecting some miracle to follow.

That night the King embraced his beloved wife and nine months later she gave birth to twins, a boy and a girl. The whole country rejoiced, knowing that the babies were blessed, and that in due course the boy would become a just and noble king and that the girl would become a beautiful and wise princess.

Nowadays people in towns don't believe in Khizr, or in miracles, but in the country he is sometimes seen in various disguises by simple folk who, of course, only realize who he is when he has vanished and their wish has been fulfilled. When all the learning in the world can't help a desperate human being, the sort of intervention from the Invisible World we call a miracle is the only hope. This is why the poet has said, 'If God closes one door through knowledge/He opens another through mercy'.[2]

We are not meant to know His ways.

The Cruel Mother-in-Law

There was one and there was none/Except for God there was no one.

The story I'm going to tell you happened a long time ago, in the North. I heard it from our village weaver who was a hundred years old, and she had learnt it from an old aunt who had forgotten how she came to know it. Perhaps it was her own life story, or perhaps she had invented it, or else it came from the *Alam-e-Gheib*, that mysterious Occult World where all stories are born. No matter.

There was a widow called Touba who lived with her only son, Hamid, in a house near the sea. At the age of barely fourteen Touba had been married off to a haberdasher, a widower whose wife had died without giving him any children. He was old enough to be Touba's father, but her parents were very poor and they were anxious to marry her off as soon as possible so they would have one less mouth to feed.

At first Touba was unhappy, her husband seemed so very old to her, but he was kind and gentle and she grew fond of him. At least she had her own house and enough to eat, and she was respected by the community. When after a year she produced Hamid

95

her husband was overjoyed — at last he had the son and heir he had longed for all his life. He sacrificed a huge sheep, bought a sack of rice and gave a lavish meal for the poor, who flocked from all the villages of the district, ate their fill and wished the new-born baby long life and prosperity.

As it happened, the new baby brought luck and the haberdasher's business flourished. He became an important member of the Bazaar and acquired a reputation for prudence and business acumen which led other traders to consult him for advice.

Time passed and Hamid grew into a nice bright boy. His father often took him to the shop, which would one day be his.

After a few years the haberdasher told his wife that he was now rich enough to be eligible for *Hajj* and that he had no choice but to fulfil his religious obligations and travel to Mecca, much as he was loath to leave her and their son. He entrusted his business to his brother, urged him to take good care of his family and left to join the caravan of pilgrims bound for Arabia.

In those days months passed before any news came from the pilgrims. The journey was hazardous: the mountains were infested with bandits who raided the caravans, killed the travellers or else took their possessions and left them stranded in the middle of the wilderness to starve to death or be eaten by wild beasts; disease and natural disasters also took their toll and sometimes there were shipwrecks in the Persian Gulf, which the pilgrims had to cross to reach the shores of Arabia and the House of God.

Touba waited for news, but weeks went by without her hearing anything. Then one day a messenger came bearing bad news: there had indeed been a storm at sea and the pilgrims' ship had sunk with everyone on board. Touba was shattered, but thanked God that at least her husband had left a prosperous business and that her brother-in-law was there to watch over her and Hamid.

'God always leaves room for thanks', as the adage goes; things could indeed be worse.

Her brother-in-law came to see her on the first day of each month to give her the money from the haberdashery but every time it was a smaller sum until there was barely enough for her to make ends meet. He made all sorts of excuses why the business was not doing well and Touba believed him, hoping that the tide would turn.

One day her brother-in-law arrived looking distraught and announced that the business had gone bankrupt, that he had closed it down and was going to the city to find work. He promised to send her some money as soon as he could.

Needless to say he was never seen or heard of again. Touba understood: either he had deliberately swindled her or else he had mismanaged the business. Whatever the case, there she was, a widow with a child and no resources. She wept and clutched her head and called upon the Prophet and the Imams for justice and succour, and in the end she knuckled down to work and began to earn a living, accepting any menial job she was offered and never complaining.

But gradually she grew bitter and hard, and resentful of those to whom Fate had dealt a better hand. They say nothing corrodes the heart more than the acid of bitterness, just as nothing clouds the mind and tarnishes the soul more than envy, and Touba was gnawed by both. Only her son was spared her dark feelings; he became the sole object of her affection and for his sake she put up with humiliation and bullying and unfair treatment, and said nothing. She hoped that Hamid would become a dutiful and hard-working son when he grew up and would make her proud.

❀

After a while one day Touba went to the Bazaar to enquire whether anyone had heard anything about her brother-in-law and lo! the haberdashery was open and done up, and an attractive, dignified middle-aged man was serving customers. She waited until he was alone and then, pretending to need some ribbons, engaged him in conversation. It emerged that he was called Mohammad and that he was from a village beyond the forest. Wanting a change and some adventure, he had come to this part of the world, to be near the sea, and he had bought the shop. He had paid a big price for it, but he was content.

Had he heard from the previous owner, Touba wondered. 'Not a word!' replied Mohammad. 'He said he would be in touch in case I needed something, but he disappeared like a jinn.'

Touba then told him her story and the haberdasher felt very sorry for her. He promised that when Hamid was a bit older he would take him on as an apprentice.

And so it came to pass. Hamid grew into a charming and courteous young man, modest and helpful. He became first an apprentice to the new haberdasher and, soon afterwards, his trusted assistant. His boss was wise as well as being a clever and prudent tradesman, and he said to him that he was now old enough to get married and that his mother should find him a suitable bride. Hamid was too shy to broach the subject with her and his boss offered to talk to her on his behalf.

He duly summoned Touba to his house and told her that, like any good mother, she should think of her son's future and find him a good, modest girl to marry. Touba felt a stab in her heart: surely after all the tribulations she had been through to bring up her son she was entitled to enjoy his undivided attention for a few years longer? So used was she to keeping her thoughts to herself that she betrayed nothing of her jealousy. 'Of course you are right,' she agreed, and Mohammad immediately suggested Samira, the daughter of one of his friends, and offered to be the go-between. The bride's father was delighted: the recommendation of the haberdasher was enough and the young man seemed gentle and thoughtful.

The wedding feast was paid for by Hamid's kind boss and the young bride moved in with Hamid and his mother. Touba was so jealous of her daughter-in-law that she could barely contain her anger and resentment, and she hatched a plot to get rid of her. Every day when Hamid left for work, Touba began to bully and badger Samira, keeping her hard at work cleaning, washing and preparing meals, making her do everything over and over again and continually criticizing her. At midday she ate a huge lunch but gave nothing to the young girl except a piece of stale bread and a glass of water. By the time Hamid came home in the evening, his young wife was exhausted and starving, but she was too proud to complain. Then when they sat down to dinner, Touba said to her son that his wife had already eaten half the food and that there was just enough left for him and herself. The poor girl would be too terrified of Touba's reprisals to protest at this lie and she went to bed hungry.

In those days the mother-in-law's authority was supreme; she ran the household and everyone obeyed her until she died, after which the daughter-in-law took her place as the mistress of the household. You might say that the girl could have run away and told her parents, but it was a question of honour — she had married for life and if she went home she would dishonour her parents; she would be considered damaged goods, no longer a virgin, and no one else would marry her. She would be a burden on her parents and despised by everyone. Besides, she loved her husband, who was tender and respectful, and she could not conceive of loving anyone else.

Gradually she lost her appetite; her rosy cheeks grew pale, her bright eyes dimmed and she became as thin as a willow wand. Her husband loved her dearly and was worried about her, but every time he tried to find out what was the matter with her, she denied that there was anything amiss. Hamid suggested a visit to the doctor, but his mother said that the doctor was a quack and that there was nothing wrong with his wife except nerves, which was natural enough in a bride, and that she'd get better soon. In the end Hamid did call the doctor, who examined the girl and prescribed some potions, but Touba stole the bottles, discarded their contents and filled them with water and vinegar, which of course had no effect on poor Samira.

Meanwhile the haberdashery was prospering and a new assistant was employed to cope with the extra work. He was called Majid and he came from Isfahan. He had been working for a dyemaker but his boss had died and the business had been sold, and Majid had decided to change his life, go somewhere else and work at a different trade. Hamid showed him the ropes and the two became fast friends.

As you know, the Isfahanis are famous for their shrewdness and wit; Majid noticed that Hamid seemed more and more preoccupied and unhappy, and one day when they were alone he asked him what the problem was. Hamid was glad to have someone in whom he could confide and he told his friend his whole story, from his father's shipwreck and his uncle's fraud to his mother's early hardships, and now his beautiful and sweet wife's wasting disease. He loved her with all his heart and the thought of losing her was unbearable to him.

His friend pondered for a moment and said, 'Leave it to me for a couple of days and I'll see what I can do.'

When Hamid arrived for work the next morning, Majid told him to mind the shop while he went off on an errand. He then went back home to his room in a house not far from Hamid's, climbed up on to the roof and, going from one roof to another, reached Hamid's house. He sat on the edge and looked down to see what was going on in the house.

He saw that Touba was bullying her daughter-in-law mercilessly, making her wash the dishes over and over again and sweep the yard ten times, all the time hitting her with a stick and telling her how ugly and useless she was. The girl cried quietly and said nothing. At lunchtime Touba sat down to a delicious bowl of *Ash* (thick soup made with rice, herbs and pulses) and some freshly baked bread, and gave nothing to Samira except a piece of mouldy bread and a glass of water, which she left untouched.

Majid went back to the shop and said to Hamid, 'You fool! Have you no eyes to see and no sense to understand what is happening to your wife? There is nothing wrong with her, she is simply starving', and he recounted all that he had witnessed from the roof.

Hamid was furious, but how could he confront his mother? He owed her everything, she had sacrificed herself for him and was now getting old — how could he show disrespect to her? She would lose face and it would make matters worse. What could he do?

'You are right,' agreed Majid. 'Nothing will be achieved by quarrelling with your mother: she is elderly and her judgement is impaired by jealousy and years of hardship. Just do as I tell you and all will be well in a short time. Go home and tell your mother that you are fed up with your wife, that it is no fun being married to a bag of bones and that you are marrying a new woman, a little older and wiser, who will appreciate her and enjoy her company.

Meanwhile you can bring your wife to my house where she will be safe with my mother and fed properly.'

Hamid agreed. That evening, when they were alone in their room, Hamid took his wife into his arms and showered her with kisses, telling her how sorry he was that he had not understood her predicament, and he explained Majid's plan to her. She was relieved and happy, and for the first time the light of hope shone in her face.

In the morning Hamid told his mother that he was tired of his malingering wife, that he was going to send her back to her parents and marry another woman, and that as a matter of fact he had found exactly the right girl, one he was sure his mother would approve of. Touba was so happy to have achieved her purpose that for a moment she almost betrayed her feelings, but she restrained herself and just said, 'Whatever you wish, my dear, is fine by me; all I ever want is your happiness.' But to herself she thought, 'I'll find a way of getting rid of your new bride as well.'

The next morning Hamid took Samira to drop her at Majid's parents' house on his way to the shop and Touba murmured, 'Good riddance!' under her breath.

In the evening Majid shaved off his beard, put on a wig and made up his face, donned a pretty, gay dress and went home with Hamid.

'Here is Moona, your new daughter-in-law,' Hamid said to his mother cheerfully.

'What a lovely bride!' exclaimed Touba, and embraced her new daughter-in-law. 'Welcome! A thousand times welcome! How glad I am to have such a graceful daughter-in-law.'

Majid pretended to be shy, smiled and kept his head bent as a sign of modesty and obedience, without removing the scarf which covered half his face. Touba thought she was even shyer and more compliant than Samira and that she would see the back of her even quicker.

She spread the *sofreh* (nap)[1] and they sat down to eat their supper. Majid took a few spoonfuls and said she was full, murmuring, 'Thank you; that was delicious.'

Touba thought, 'Well, this one will be even easier to deal with: she doesn't have much appetite to start with.'

When they were alone in their nuptial room, Hamid and Majid locked the door and had a good laugh, but Hamid was still anxious.

In the morning he left for work, telling his mother to take good care of his new wife. As soon as he was gone Touba told the girl to tie on her apron and get to work, but she refused: 'I'm a bride, I don't want my husband to come home and find me dirty; you clean the house yourself.'

Touba was speechless! How dared this young woman disobey her? She picked up her stick to hit her hard on the head, but Majid grabbed it in the air, broke it in two against his knee in one blow and threw it at her.

'Now, you get to work before I break the stick on your head,' he said. 'And get everything done quickly: I want my lunch at midday sharp!'

Touba was so frightened that she started sweeping the yard, vowing to sort things out with her son when he came home in the evening. Meanwhile Majid ordered her about, criticized everything she did, asked her to wash the lavatory five times over and finally told her to cook lunch and serve it. When the tray of food was brought to the room, Majid sat down and ate it all, leaving nothing for Touba: 'Here is a piece of bread. Wipe my plate with it for gravy.'

In the evening Majid washed and made up his face, put on a pretty dress and greeted his husband with a modest, warm smile.

'How was your day, my dear Moona?' Hamid asked him.

'Perfect. Your mother was so kind to me; she showed me everything and wouldn't let me do anything, saying that I was a bride and should keep myself clean and fresh for you.'

Touba could not believe her ears. What cheek! So young and so crafty! She didn't utter a word and waited for an opportunity to be alone with her son and tell him the truth, but this never came — the bride followed her husband wherever he went.

When Touba went to bed, Majid told Hamid how the day had been spent and that before long he would make Touba regret her gentle Samira and curse the day she decided to get rid of her.

As soon as Hamid was out of the door the next day, Majid told Touba to heat some water so that he could wash himself at home as he didn't feel like going to the *Hammam*. Well, he could hardly do that, could he? How could he go to the men's baths dressed as a woman and covered in make-up? And in the women's baths he would be exposed immediately and beaten to bits. Before Touba could protest that she was not a servant and that it was beneath her dignity to prepare the bath for her daughter-in-law, Majid gave her a sharp kick on the shin and said, 'There will be lots more of those if you don't hurry up.'

Touba began to think that her new daughter-in-law was the Devil's disciple sent down to earth to torment her; she had been mean and nasty to that poor girl who was as sweet and gentle as a lamb, who had done her no harm and whom she had driven almost to her grave, and now she was being punished for it. She was so racked with remorse that she began to cry, whereupon Majid told her to stop snivelling and get on with it or else.

When the water was ready, Majid sent Touba out shopping so that she couldn't spy on him and discover his secret. He shaved and cleaned himself, put on new clothes and made up his face. At lunchtime again he ate all the food, and to make sure Touba had nothing to eat he gave what was left to the cat, leaving nothing on the tray except a piece of bread.

Touba was determined to tell Hamid everything as soon as he arrived, but Hamid pretended to have a headache, locked himself up with his wife in their room and left in the morning without giving his mother the opportunity to open her mouth.

After a few days, when Majid felt that Touba had learnt her lesson and had been punished enough, he told Hamid to send a messenger to the house to say that Moona's mother was taken ill and that she should go to her at once.

This he did: shortly before Hamid came home there was a knock on the door and a young boy brought news that Moona's mother was at death's door and that she had to rush to her bedside. Majid pretended to be distraught, told Touba to tell her husband that she might not be back for a few days and dashed out.

He went straight to the shop and told Hamid that everything had worked out according to plan, that his mother was ready to eat humble pie and that it was now up to him to play his final cards right.

When Hamid came home, his mother brought in his supper and began to complain about his new wife, telling him what a ruthless harpy Moona was, how she had starved, bullied and beaten her.

Hamid pretended to be surprised, shocked, angry. 'I will divorce her at once and she will never come back to this house,' he said. 'But I must have a wife, a good woman who can give me some children and take care of you in your old age. So who do you wish me to marry?'

'Bring back Samira, your first bride!' Touba exclaimed. 'She was as gentle as a dove and I was not good to her.'

Again her son pretended to be astonished at such a confession, but agreed to go and see if he could persuade Samira to come back.

And so the clever Isfahani's stratagem worked. Hamid was united with his beloved Samira, and Touba cherished her for her goodness and treated her as a daughter. As for Majid, he married Samira's sister, and they all lived happily ever after.

The Lazy Wife

There was one and there was none/Except for God there was no one.

They say that a man is lazy out of cowardice, but when a woman is work-shy you have to look for some other reason. Let me tell you the story of Habiba, a young woman in Kirman who was so lazy that from one day to the next she hardly moved. She had not always been listless, far from it. As a child she was vivacious and tomboyish; she did not stand still one minute, she could not see a tree without climbing it like a monkey and she always led other children in their games and mischief. Sometimes her mother tied Habiba to herself to keep her quiet and stop her running around. They used to call her 'Habiba the lizard' because she was always darting about.

One day when Habiba was nearly thirteen and approaching puberty, her mother sat her down to give her a good talking to, telling her that she had better calm down and prepare herself for marriage; that soon a suitable husband would be found for her and that before long she would have children of her own, who would doubtless be as naughty and tear-about as she herself, and then she would understand what her mother felt.

Habiba had no wish to be grown-up, to give up fun and games for domestic chores and worries, but she knew that she had no say in the matter. Even before she reached puberty the neighbourhood began talking and matchmaking, and the marriage-broker got busy. No matter how much Habiba protested, no matter how much she wanted to stay with her mother a little longer, it was all to no avail: the sooner a girl got married, the better her chances of making a good match. If she turned down a suitable offer, people would begin to whisper that there was something wrong with her and before you knew where you were she would be past twenty and might stay on the shelf forever, to the shame of her family and her own eternal regret.

So it was that from among Habiba's suitors her parents chose Taher, a young man who was known to be quiet and industrious.

In those days a newly married couple lived with the husband's family until they had children. But Taher had no family; his parents had died when he was young, and a coppersmith in the Bazaar had taken him under his wing and made him his apprentice. He was now the coppersmith's trusted assistant and it was understood that in due course, when his boss grew old and retired, he would take over the shop. For a long time he had lived in a cabin behind the shop, but he was prudent and had saved up his money, and recently he had bought himself a little house nearby, in anticipation of matrimony.

Taher was happy to be getting married to a girl who by all accounts was not only pretty but spirited and gay, so happy he could hardly wait. He decorated his little house and made it more comfortable, and he spent much of his savings on a lavish wedding feast. On the wedding night he waited impatiently for the guests to leave and leave him alone with his bride.

He found Habiba shy and unresponsive to his advances, but that was natural modesty, he thought, and very becoming in a young girl. He tried to make her relax by talking to her gently, but whatever he said, she just shook her head. Eventually she crouched in a corner and fell asleep.

Taher was disappointed but not unduly worried — after all she was only fourteen, and soon she would get used to him and her new environment and all would be well. The next day he went to work, reluctant to leave Habiba alone, and rushed back home at sunset, wondering how she had fared in his absence. Doubtless she had cleaned the house and prepared a nice meal for them.

To his surprise he found her sitting in the same spot where she had left her, and nothing had been touched.

'What is the matter, my dear?' he asked her anxiously.

'Nothing,' she replied. 'I'm frightened.'

'Frightened of what?' he wondered, but she kept repeating 'I'm frightened', and refused to budge.

Taher was a kind, patient young man, and he said to himself that Habiba was daunted by the prospect of married life, and that soon she would get over her fear and grow fond of him. He cleared up the breakfast dishes, put on the *samovar* and made tea, cooking their dinner at the same time. When everything was ready he spread the *sofreh*, brought the food in and they sat down to eat. To his delight Habiba ate with great appetite, relishing every morsel, and at the end she even wiped her plate clean with a piece of bread.

After the meal Taher expected her to clear up, fold up the nap and put it away, and wash up the dishes, but Habiba crawled back to her corner and said, 'I'm frightened!'

'There is nothing to be frightened of,' Taher reassured her. 'I'm with you and nothing bad can happen to you.'

'I'm frightened,' she repeated, and didn't move.

So Taher took care of everything before going to bed.

Days passed, then weeks, then months, and Habiba refused to do any work whatsoever; every time her husband asked her to do something, she refused, saying, 'I'm frightened.' Even if Taher asked for a bowl of water, she said, 'Get it yourself, I'm frightened.' Taher tried to reason with her, but it was no good. And of course there was no question of intimacy: as soon as Taher made the slightest move to touch her, she began whimpering and trembling and curling up against the wall like a scared kitten. He began to wonder if Habiba would ever change: even if she never did any work would she at least allow him to get close to her and cuddle her? He was in a quandary — she was beautiful and he loved her, he didn't want to do what any other young man in his place would do and send her back to her parents, he was too proud to tell his boss and ask his advice, and he had no one else to turn to.

Then one day his boss was ill and Taher had to go to another town to deliver some goods. He left enough food for Habiba, and hoped that she would be all right in his absence. After two days he came back and found that Habiba had eaten everything, but left all the dirty dishes unwashed. 'I'm frightened,' she said as soon as he came in, and didn't move.

Taher became despondent. His predicament seemed hopeless. He worked hard all day, and every evening, instead of a welcoming wife and a hot meal, he found a quivering bird crouched in a corner, twittering, 'I'm frightened, I'm frightened.' What was the solution, he wondered. He could not think of any.

One evening he found Habiba in an unusually happy mood. She told him that her cousin was getting married and that she had been invited to the wedding. It so happened that one of her aunts had married a rich draper, and they were giving their daughter a grand wedding party.

In those days a wedding lasted nearly a week — a few days of preparations followed by three days of ceremonies during which the women of the bride's family were invited to stay at her house and help. When everything was ready the festivities began. The first day the bride was taken to the *Hammam* with the other women of the family, scrubbed and washed by a *dallak* (bath attendant) until her skin glowed, and henna was applied to her hair, fingers and toes. The next day the Mullah came and performed the wedding ritual and the marriage contract was signed. Finally on the third day the wedding feast took place, with musicians and dancers and abundant food, starting with tea in the afternoon and ending with dinner late in the evening. Of course all this was for the better off; the poor just did their best with whatever they could afford.

Habiba was so glad to be going away for a few days that she almost forgot to say 'I'm frightened' when her husband came home.

Taher noticed her change of mood and was perplexed. He too was invited to the wedding feast with the other men of the family, but he refused, saying that he could not get away, as his boss was going off on business again and he would be in charge of the shop. This was an excuse; the real reason was that he felt forlorn at his predicament and wanted to stay behind and think.

Once Habiba had left and he was on his own, Taher pondered what to do with his wife. She had become happy and vivacious when she knew she was leaving the house, and he wondered how she would behave when she was with her family and friends. He asked his boss for a couple of days off and travelled to the town where the wedding was taking place.

By the time he arrived and found the house of Habiba's uncle it was late, the sun had set and the festivities were in full swing. Instead of going in with the other guests, Taher went to the nearby mosque, climbed on to the roof and walked along the ledges until he reached the roof of the house next door to the uncle's, from which he had a commanding view of the wedding party. And what a party!

There was a vast garden, lit with lanterns hung from trees. The large pool in the middle had been covered with planks and carpeted to make a dance floor, and on it were dancing beautiful women in diaphanous silk dresses. Sitting to one side were musicians playing enchanting music. The guests, the men on the right, the women on the left, a row of poplars making a screen between them, sat at tables covered with plates of sweetmeats and pastries and cornucopias of fruit. Crowds of servants milled around filling glasses with a variety of iced sherbets and replenishing the plates. This was merely the preliminary to the dinner, which would be served later; delicious aromas were already wafting from the kitchen as far as the roof-top.

Taher looked for his wife and spotted her among the guests. Surrounded by a group of young women, Habiba seemed to be the heart and soul of the party, talking and laughing. He moved a little closer, wanting to hear what they were saying. It appeared that the discussion was about courage: how some people were timid and others daring, some cowardly and others brave, and how the latter were more attractive, always the winners in life as well as in games. They told stories and quoted poetry and proverbs to illustrate the argument.

'Nothing dared, nothing gained,' Habiba ventured, and everyone agreed with the adage. 'I don't know what fear is,' continued Habiba. 'I'm so fearless that I can go to the cemetery at night, when all the ghosts come out, and cook *halva* (sweetmeat made with flour, butter, sugar and saffron) and make merry, regardless of the darkness, the howling wind and the prowling spirits.'

The others laughed and dared her to do it that very night, saying that if she went to the cemetery and came back with her *halva*, they would each give her a piece of jewellery. One pledged an emerald pendant, another a sapphire ring, yet another a pair of ruby earrings. Habiba accepted the challenge immediately and the young women rushed to get the necessary utensils and ingredients from the kitchen — a pot and a large spoon, flour, butter, sugar and saffron.

Taher was stunned. What a fool he had been! To think that he had believed his wife was a fragile little creature afraid of everything! But he had no time to waste in regret. He rushed back along the roofs, reached the mosque and climbed down, and ran to the cemetery as fast as he could.

The cemetery was in the middle of the woods on a deserted island in a lake not far from the town; only a narrow causeway connected the island to the shore. No one dared go to the island, especially at night, for fear of wild animals, but Taher swallowed his fear and ran fast so he would get there before his wife.

It was a starry night, the rows of tombs stretched out to the edge of the forest, and the trees cast dark shadows on the tombstones, shadows that moved as the breeze shook the branches. Now and again the silence was broken by the flapping of wings or the hooting of an owl. It was so spooky that every time a shadow moved Taher was startled, afraid a panther or a wild boar would jump on him from behind. But he was determined to catch his wife out. He looked around and found a white sack which he tore up and wrapped around himself like a shroud. Then he lay down near the entrance by an empty tomb, pretending to be a corpse left there for burial the next day.

Presently Habiba arrived with her pot and ingredients, and put them on a tombstone near the corpse. In no time at all she collected some wood and twigs, lit a fire and began to cook. She sang as she churned the pot and soon a delicious smell of roasting flour filled the air. Taher marvelled at his wife's efficiency and fearlessness, and for the first time since his wedding the balm of hope soothed his bruised heart. If he could have this real Habiba for his wife he would be a happy man.

When the *halva* was ready and Habiba prepared to leave, he stretched out his arm and said, 'Can I have some? The living must take care/To give the dead their share.'

Instead of screaming with terror and fainting at the sight of a corpse demanding a portion of her *halva*, Habiba hit the stretched hand hard with her red-hot spoon and said, 'This spoon is what I need/To give you for your greed!'

Taher suppressed a cry of pain and stretched out his other arm. 'The living must take care/To give the dead their share,' he repeated, and again Habiba dealt a burning blow to his hand with the hot spoon.

To her surprise the corpse wasn't subdued, but uncovered its chest and said, 'The living must take care/To give the dead their share.'

Habiba then struck its chest so hard that it took Taher's breath away. 'Here is the share of a greedy ghost!' she said, and without further ado she picked up her pot and ran across the causeway and back to the party.

Meanwhile her companions waited for Habiba's return, and as time passed and there was no sign of her, they began to fret. They regretted having challenged her and wondered what they should do. As they were arguing, Habiba came in. At the sight of her they cheered with relief and delight; they embraced her and then devoured her *halva*, which they pronounced the most scrumptious they had ever tasted. Not only was Habiba intrepid, she was also an expert cook, and they were proud of her; they gladly gave her the pieces of jewellery they had wagered.

Now let me tell you about Taher. He went home in great pain and discomfort on account of his burns. He put some ointment on his chest and hands and pondered what to do next. What a crafty little vixen he had married, he mused, and couldn't help admiring her. To think that she had fooled him for months with her pretend modesty and childish fears.

The next day Habiba came home and when Taher arrived from work in the evening, he found her crouching in her usual corner, hugging her knees against her chest, as listless, pale and sad-eyed as ever.

'God is great!' he murmured to himself. 'What a weird situation I'm in!' Where was the beautiful young woman with glowing skin, thrilling laughter and bubbling talk he had seen at the wedding? What was the meaning of her strange behaviour?

He pretended not to notice anything untoward, and said, 'I'm tired tonight, so you are going to cook us some supper, perhaps even a little *halva*, to celebrate your homecoming.'

Habiba whimpered, 'I can't, I'm frightened.'

Taher could not hold out any longer and he burst out, 'You were not afraid to go to the cemetery in the middle of the forest on a desolate island at night and cook *halva* for your friends, but you are afraid to go into the kitchen of your own house and prepare some food for your husband?'

And he opened his shirt and showed her the burns on his chest and his hands. Habiba realized that the corpse she called 'a greedy ghost' was her own long-suffering husband, and before Taher had time to issue any threats, she threw herself into his arms and begged his forgiveness. She explained that in the beginning she had wanted to test his affection and his patience, but then she had got into the habit of pretending and she did not know how to stop or alter her behaviour without giving the game away. She knew now that her husband was the kindest of men and she the luckiest of women, and she swore to be an exemplary wife for the rest of their lives.

And so she was — clever, quick, gay. She cooked him delicious meals and kept their house spotless. Taher's patience and gentleness had paid off and Habiba was indeed lucky not to lose her husband. But it is dangerous to put a heart to the test — it could break irremediably, and leave you with regret and remorse forever.

In time Taher's boss retired and he took over the shop, engaged an assistant and life became easier. He and Habiba had several children and were very happy.

The Man Whose Luck
Had Gone to Sleep

There was one and there was none/Except for God there was no one.

Once upon a time there was a young man called Qassem, who lived with his mother in a village on the edge of the desert in the South. This young man was famous in the whole region for being the laziest and most idle person anyone had ever known. He did nothing all day and slept most of the time; he only managed to shake himself awake in order to eat. His father had died when he was a child and his mother had worked in the fields as a hired hand to earn a meagre living and bring him up as best she could. She hoped that when he grew up and she became old he would take care of them both.

Instead as time passed Qassem became more and more lazy, until he hardly got out of bed. Every morning the *Muezzin* called the faithful to prayer and everyone got up to pray and then go to work, but Qassem lingered in bed until noon. His mother left him something for lunch and when she came home at sunset she found him reclining in his bed or sitting in a corner, waiting for her to

117

arrive and cook their dinner. And no sooner had she cleared up the dishes than Qassem crawled back into his bed.

In those days it was customary that when the father died, the eldest son, as long as he had reached puberty, became the bread-winner and head of the family. But Qassem refused to assume his responsibilities, and whenever his mother told him he should get a job and earn a living, he replied, 'I'll not succeed, because my Luck has gone to sleep,[1] and until it wakes up I can't do anything.'

Time passed. Qassem's mother began to think that her son would never work and she became very worried; she was getting old, her work on the land was heavy and uncertain, and any day she might succumb to some illness and die. Worse still she could be afflicted with an ailment that would cripple her and put her out of action. How would they survive then? But whenever she broached the subject of work with her son, he said, 'My Luck has gone to sleep; until it wakes up again I will never succeed in anything I undertake, so what's the point of trying?'

In desperation his mother went to see the village Mullah and explain her predicament, and the Mullah agreed to have a chat with the young man. One day when she was out working he went to see Qassem. He told him that this was no life for a young man, always cooped up in a room, listless and lonely, and he reminded the son of his duty to his mother, who had toiled hard to bring him up and who was now getting old and frail. He finally urged him to pull himself together and go out and look for a job.

'What is the point?' Qassem responded. 'My Luck has gone to sleep. I shall only fail at whatever I do.'

The Mullah offered to find him a very easy job, one so easy that success would be guaranteed — he could help the grain mer-chant in the Bazaar, for example, mind the shop in his absence and shift the sacks of grain, that sort of thing. As it happened the grain merchant was looking for an assistant and the Mullah could have a word with him.

'I prefer to wait for my Luck to wake up,' said Qassem. 'Then I will get a proper job and make lots of money.'

The Mullah decided that this was just Qassem's excuse, that really he was just bone lazy, and he gave up on him.

After that it was the turn of the village elders to talk to Qassem and persuade him to do something and earn a living. Then it was the turn of the young men of his own age, all of whom were working. All of them had married and started families, while he himself just wasted his youth staying in bed, waiting for his Luck to wake up and come knocking on the door with fame and fortune on a gold plate.

Now there was an old weaver in the village, a kind, benevolent woman as ancient as the hills. She sat at her loom all day weaving and gave her cloth to the draper in the Bazaar to sell. No one remembered how old she was, but everyone liked and respected her, for she was wise and friendly, and always ready to give the benefit of her long experience of life to whoever confided in her or sought her advice. When Qassem's mother turned to her and told her about her son, she listened carefully and after pondering the situation she said, 'I'll come and see him when you are out, and we'll see what happens.'

A few days later the old weaver knocked at the cottage door at noon, when she knew Qassem would be up eating his lunch, and he let her in. Instead of mentioning work she talked about the price of cotton and the latest news from town, and finally said, 'I hear that your Luck has gone to sleep. Is that true?' Qassem admitted that it was, and the old weaver said, 'Well, years ago I knew a young man whose Luck had gone to sleep, and you know what he did?' Qassem said he did not. 'He went and found his Luck and woke him up,' said the old woman, 'and lo and behold, his life changed, and soon he was one of the most successful and prosperous men in the district. You must do the same: go and find your Luck and wake him up, otherwise he could remain asleep forever and ruin your life.'

'What a brilliant idea!' exclaimed Qassem. 'Why, it's so obvious this is exactly what I must do! How stupid of me not to have thought of it before.'

He thanked the old weaver profusely and promised to leave the very next morning and search for his Luck.

That evening when his mother came home Qassem told her about the old weaver's visit and his own plan to go and find his Luck wherever he might be and wake him up. His mother was delighted and for the first time in years mother and son went to bed in high hopes.

The next day at dawn the mother prepared a bundle of food and a gourd of water for her son, and Qassem set off on his journey. Soon he had left the village behind; ahead lay a long road snaking through the wilderness, twisting round bare hills and scorched plains, and disappearing into the hazy horizon. He kept walking until the sun was high in the sky and he knew it was midday.

Presently he saw a little oasis, a few trees casting their shadow on a glassy pool, birds singing among the branches, a gentle breeze rustling the leaves. He was hot and hungry, and he thought he would sit down under a tree for a few minutes and have something to eat. He took some bread and cheese from his bundle, drank a draught of water from his gourd and lay down to have a little snooze.

But before he had closed his eyes he heard a mighty growl followed by a roar, and turning his head he saw a huge lion rounding a boulder and slinking towards him. Qassem was petrified —

that was surely the end of him! Instead of finding his Luck, he was going to be torn to pieces and eaten by a lion.

To his amazement the lion started talking to him. 'Don't be afraid,' he said. 'I won't hurt you, but I need your help. I am the king of the animals in this desert and I have been keeping my kingdom in good order, with justice and prudence. But now I am getting old and I feel my brain is going soft,[2] which is the worst disease any creature could possibly catch. I must find a cure for it quickly, before the animals notice and some smart upstart tries to challenge my authority. Do you know a cure for it?'

Qassem was very sorry, he did not. 'I'm looking for my Luck, because he has gone to sleep and I want to find him and wake him up so that my life can change for the better.'

'In that case,' said the lion, 'I'll let you go, but on condition that when you find your Luck you ask him what is the cure for a brain that has gone soft, and come back to tell me.'

Qassem promised he would, and without any further delay took to the road again, glad to have escaped certain death.

He walked and walked, always on the lookout for his Luck, but without ever seeing a living soul. Presently he came across a stream; the water gushed forth from under the rocks and ran west towards the setting sun. He stopped to drink and wash his face. As he put his hand in the cool crystalline water, the stream began to talk. 'Where are you heading, young man?' it asked, and Qassem explained his purpose. 'Go ahead,' said the good water, 'and may God protect you and help you find your Luck.'

Qassem filled his gourd from the stream water and went on his way. Gradually the sky grew grey; the celestial dome began to glitter with stars, the Milky Way arched to the horizon and soon the desert was plunged into darkness.

Qassem kept walking, and turning a bend he suddenly found himself in front of a magnificent castle lit with a myriad lights. Surely this was a mirage or hallucination brought on by fatigue, but no, it was real, for he heard a sweet voice calling out to him, 'Welcome, wayfarer, come in and be our guest.'

He looked up, and there at the window of the tower were two ravishing young girls, one blonde and the other brunette, scintillating in their lovely attire and smiling at him. Presently the gates opened and a dozen servants rushed forward with a chair to carry him in. He was hungry and tired and longed to go in and be given food and shelter, but he remembered his purpose.

'I am sorry,' he said to the young girls. 'I'm on my way to find my Luck who has gone to sleep and wake him up, and much as I would like to stay with you in your beautiful castle, I can't tarry.'

The young girls laughed and ran away, the gates closed and Qassem continued walking. After a few steps he looked back in regret to see if the girls were back at the window, but the castle had vanished and all around him was nothing but the dark, empty desert.

Soon the stars began to fade and a milky light diffused in the air, dawn broke, and a huge walnut tree appeared on the side of the road. He sat down in its shade to rest a little while and as he leaned against the trunk the tree began to talk.

'Where are you going young man?' it asked.

'I'm looking for my Luck,' Qassem replied and the walnut tree wished him a safe journey.

Around noon he came across a little man lying in the shade of a lone wild oak beside a little spring, fast asleep. At his approach the man woke up and smiled at him as if he knew him.

'Who are you?' asked Qassem. 'And what are you doing in this God-forsaken wilderness?'

'I'm your Luck,' said the man. 'I was expecting you, and I thought I'd get some sleep while I waited.'

Qassem jumped for joy! He could not believe that he had at last reached his destination and found his Luck. What was he to do now, he wondered.

'How glad I am to see you!' he exclaimed. 'I have been walking for days, lost in this desert, looking everywhere for you and I was beginning to give up hope of ever finding you. Now let us go back home, for my mother must be worrying.'

'Sit down,' said his Luck. 'Have something to eat and rest your feet, then we'll make our way back.'

Qassem had exhausted his provisions, but his Luck gave him some delicious bread and meat and a cup of cool sherbet, and after Qassem had rested and washed his feet, he said to him, 'Now walk back the same way as you came and I will be right behind you. But beware! I will give you three chances. If you understand and seize them I'll stay with you forever, but if you miss them through arrogance or stubbornness, then I will disappear and go back to sleep forever, and you'll never find me again.'

Qassem agreed to the deal readily — after all, how could he possibly go wrong with his Luck right behind him?

Just as they were setting out he remembered the promise he had made to the old lion and asked his Luck, 'By the way, what is the cure for a lion whose brain has gone soft?'

'The only cure is to eat the brain of the most stupid human being he can find,' his Luck replied and they started their return journey.

Qassem was so happy to have found his Luck and woken him up that he was almost flying. With his Luck behind him he could undertake anything and everything he touched would turn to gold.

Now and again he looked back to reassure himself that his Luck was keeping up with him and sure enough the funny little man was there, a few steps behind him, smiling.

After a while they reached the ancient walnut tree where Qassem had rested. The tree recognized and saluted him, saying, 'I can see that you have found your Luck. Don't hurry away, sit down and rest a while. There is an axe in the hollow of my trunk where the big branches divide. Pick it up and dig the ground around my roots, and you will find a buried treasure, a huge pot full of gold sovereigns and precious stones.'

Qassem declined, saying, 'I'm sorry, but I have no time to waste on speculation about buried treasures. Now that I have found my Luck and woken him up, I must hurry home and make my fortune.'

And without further argument he hurried away, his Luck hard on his heels.

They walked on and on until the sun went down and they arrived at the illuminated castle shining like the *Gohar-Shab-Cheraq* against the darkening sky. The two beautiful young gazelles, one blonde, the other brunette, rushed forward to greet Qassem, saying, 'This time you must stay. Our father has passed away and you can marry both of us and become the Knight and master of his domain; and all his land and riches will belong to you and its people will become your loyal subjects.'

Qassem was so tempted that he was about to accept with alacrity, but he suddenly saw his Luck, standing behind him, smiling, and he said, 'You do me great honour, ladies, but alas I can't accept, for I have my Luck with me and I must go home and try to make my fortune, otherwise he might run away and go to sleep again.' Saying this, he bade them farewell regretfully and walked away, his Luck following behind, smiling.

Finally they reached the talking stream and stopped to drink some water, and the stream said to Qassem, 'Walk a furlong along my course and you'll come upon a little dam made with rocks and pebbles to form a pool. Beside it is a willow tree and if you dig under it you'll find a large treasure, a chest full of jewellery and gold vessels.'

Qassem said, 'I have no time for such an uncertain enterprise — I have my Luck with me and I must go home as soon as possible and get on with my life, otherwise he might get angry and go back to sleep again.'

Saying this he began to walk on, but his Luck stopped him. 'I told you I would give you three chances, and that if you did not seize them I would leave you, this time for good. Three times since the start of our journey you have been offered great fortune and the fulfilment of all your heart's desires, and each time you have turned this down. Instead of seizing the moment and being grateful, you were greedy and impatient, and you thought you knew best. From now on you'll have to work hard to gain a fraction of what was offered to you free.'

And before Qassem had time to apologize and promise to be less thoughtless and arrogant, his Luck had vanished. He looked around and found nothing but the infinite wilderness. He was stunned by despair at his own blindness and greed, then he picked himself up and began to walk.

He walked on forlornly until he reached the little oasis and he sat down in the shade and began to cry. Presently he heard a thundering roar and saw the old lion approaching. This time he was not afraid, for at least he had an answer for the lion's illness.

'Did you find your Luck?' asked the old lion.

Qassem said he had and that he had not forgotten to ask him about a cure for softness of the brains. 'My Luck said that you must find the most stupid man in the world, kill him and eat his brain, and that is the only remedy for your illness.'

The lion asked him what had happened to his Luck and Qassem told him the whole story from beginning to end: how he had indeed found his Luck and woken him up, how his Luck had given him three chances, and how out of greed and impatience he had lost them all. Now his Luck had vanished for good and he was disconsolate.

The lion listened to his tale and said, 'It is obvious that I shall never find a more stupid man than you, so I should kill you and eat your brain to heal my own.' Saying this he pulled in his paws and crouched as if about to pounce on his prey, but then he stopped and said, 'I could kill you and eat your brain, but I won't, because in fact my head is perfectly sound. I just wanted to test you. Because you kept your promise and brought me an answer, I'll let you go. But you must promise to give up your laziness and get down to work like everybody else. Your Luck has not gone away for good, he has just made himself invisible, but every time you take advantage of an opportunity, he will be there, right behind you.'

Qassem thanked the old lion for sparing his life and for giving him good advice, and he walked away.

After a couple of days he reached his village and went straight home where his mother was anxiously waiting for his return. Soon news spread that Qassem was back and everybody came to see him and hear about his long journey. Qassem never told anyone about his adventures, only that he had indeed found his Luck and woken him up. But the old weaver guessed what had happened because Qassem started working at the grain merchant's shop. He worked hard and made the business prosper, and in due course his boss made him his heir and left him everything to retire to a life of prayer and contemplation. Qassem married a lovely girl, almost as beautiful as the princesses he had seen in the magic castle, and they lived happily and had many children. Every time some thing good happened to him, he remembered the funny little man he had found in the wilderness, but he didn't need to look round to see if his Luck was there behind him, smiling — he knew he was.

I Know That Already

There was one and there was none/Except for God there was no one.

There was a young girl in Rasht called Qamar, which as you know is one of the names of the moon, and which suited her, for she was very pretty. God in his infinite wisdom endows everybody with some gift and he had given Qamar good looks but not much sense. She was slow on the uptake, tactless and intrusive; all too often she would comment on people's imperfections or ask them indiscreet questions. Her mother urged her to 'chew her words twice', as they say, before opening her mouth, but she was too feather-brained to pay attention.

Qamar's parents were afraid that she might stay on the shelf, despite her pretty face, and so they married her off to the first suitor who came along. Her husband was a young apprentice tanner, who was decent, good-looking and far from work-shy, and everyone said how lucky Qamar was to have made such a good match.

In those days daughters helped their mothers with their daily chores almost as soon as they could walk, and they learnt cooking and housekeeping in the process, but Qamar was too scatterbrained to learn the subtleties of preparing ingredients and concocting delectable dishes, and her mother soon gave up on her. As long as Qamar helped with housekeeping and cleaning her mother was content, and she hoped that when her daughter married, her mother-in-law might have better luck with her. As it happened Qamar's husband had lost his mother and he lived with his old father, so the young bride found herself the mistress of the household; she had to cook not only for her husband but for her father-in-law as well.

In those days there were no cookery books or classes; you learnt from your elders as you went along, and if you tasted some new dish and liked it, you asked the person who had cooked it to explain how they'd made it.

The first day of her married life Qamar asked her husband what he would like for his dinner and he tactfully chose something simple.

'A tasty *Ab-gousht* (lamb soup)[1] would be welcome,' he ventured gently. 'Do you know how to make it?'

'Of course I do,' Qamar replied, and having heard that the way to a man's heart is through his stomach, she added, 'As a matter of fact I'm a keen cook and I plan to make a variety of delicious meals for you.'

Her husband was pleased and left for work happy, already rubbing his tummy in anticipation of the evening meal.

Qamar of course didn't have a clue how to make *Ab-gousht* or anything else. What to do? They had a neighbour, an elderly widow who had offered to help the young bride if ever she needed anything. So, as soon as her husband left for work Qamar went to her cottage and asked her how to cook an *Ab-gousht*. The widow explained how you put the shank of mutton with an onion, some chickpeas and beans in water and let them cook slowly; how you add the seasoning, salt and pepper and dried lime, and so on. At every step, Qamar said, 'I know that already, what next?' She did not want to admit that she was an ignoramus, and instead of thanking the old widow for her kind explanations, she pretended that she knew everything already and that she simply wanted to compare their recipes.

Now the old widow was kind and experienced, and she made allowances for the arrogance of youth. Instead of saying to Qamar, 'If you are such a know-all why ask me?', she explained every detail patiently and clearly to make sure that the result would be a successful *Ab-gousht* — not as easy as it seems, I might add — and endear Qamar even more to her husband and her father-in-law. Sure enough Qamar managed to make a reasonable *Ab-gousht* and honour was saved.

For the next couple of days Qamar managed with the rest of the mashed chickpeas and beans, but the third day was Thursday (the eve of the Sabbath) and her husband asked if they could have some saffron rice with *fessenjan* (stew).[2] Qamar agreed with alacrity, saying that it was one of her specialities.

As soon as her husband left the house she dashed to her neighbour's cottage and asked her how to cook the rice and the stew, and again the old widow explained to her every step and went over it several times to make sure that Qamar understood. Yet after every sentence, Qamar said, 'Oh I know that already. What next?'

This went on for a long time. Every day Qamar asked her husband what he wanted for dinner and he suggested some favourite dish, and as soon as he had gone she knocked on the old widow's door to ask how to make it. But everybody knows that it is not so much the recipe that makes food delicious as the *hand* of the cook; the same dish made by two separate cooks can taste completely different — in one case delectable, in the other bland. Then there is what we call the 'breath of the glass-blower',[3] that subtle extra something which cannot be explained. Two glass-makers can set out to make identical vases and the result will be slightly different. So the dishes that Qamar made were not as good as the old widow's concoctions, far from it, but they were adequate and her husband was content.

Her good neighbour knew about human nature and its twists, and she did not expect gratitude from Qamar, but some acknowledgement of her unstinting helpfulness was surely in order. Also if she did not mind Qamar's thoughtlessness, others would, and sooner or later she would come a cropper. So she decided to teach her young neighbour a lesson.

It was early summer and the season of cherries. Qamar's husband expressed a desire for a sour-cherry pilau, and Qamar went to see the old widow and ask her how to make it. The widow explained how you pitted the sour cherries and cooked them with sugar, mixed the concoction with rice, added the tiny meatballs and steamed the pilau, and after every step Qamar said, 'Oh I know that already. What next?'

At the end the old widow said, 'The last and most important thing, "the glass-blower's breath", is to put a large cow-pat on the rice, cover the pot and let it steam.'

'Oh I know that already,' Qamar replied and without further ado ran to the fields where the cattle grazed, picked a large cow-pat and took it home. She prepared the rice and cherries and before putting the mixture to steam into a pilau, she pressed the cow-pat on top of the rice.

In the evening her husband came home, hungry and looking forward to the cherry pilau. Qamar told him that he would find that she had excelled herself, for she had added a special detail which nobody else knew and which would make the pilau exceptionally tasty.

When she brought the pot in and lifted the cover to serve, a pungent smell of cow-dung rose from the pot: the cow-pat had melted and seeped through the pot. The rice looked as disgusting as it smelt.

Qamar's husband could not believe his eyes, or his nose, wondering whether his wife had taken leave of her senses. Qamar was forced to explain what had happened and the two of them went to see the old widow.

'Why did you do this to me?' asked the mortified Qamar.

The widow explained that she had been forced to take such a step in order to make Qamar understand the hard way. Otherwise she would go through life being tactless, and the next person who did her a favour without receiving an acknowledgement might hit her much harder than she ever would.

Husband and wife apologized profusely and Qamar promised to mend her ways. The old widow forgave her and promised to be always patient and available to help her.

And so gradually Qamar became a good cook, making her husband and her children content.

You see, it costs nothing to say 'Thank you', but it makes life sweeter.

The Good Vizir and His Pride

There was one and there was none/Except for God there was no one.

T he story I am about to tell you goes back centuries, perhaps a thousand years, to when Persia was ruled by a great king called Soltan Mahmoud.[1] He conquered many lands and reigned over a vast and rich kingdom. After he had vanquished all his enemies and pacified the whole country, he settled down in his capital Ghazneh, where he established a magnificent court whose splendour surpassed that of the Khan of China. Poets and savants were drawn to it from all over the country, and learning and the arts flourished under his patronage. After his death, legends and stories proliferated about him and his magnificent Court, some true and some invented, and they have lived on to this day. Among them is the story I'm going to tell you tonight.

Soltan Mahmoud had a grand vizir called Naseem, whom he loved wholeheartedly and trusted completely. In this he showed good judgement, for Naseem was an exceptional man and much loved by the people on account of his wisdom, piety, compassion and generosity. As the Grand Vizir and confidant of the King he wielded great power, which he used judiciously. Under his administration the country prospered and the inhabitants were content.

But who was Naseem? He was the son of a poor shepherd, who had spent his childhood helping his father to mind a small flock of goats and sheep. As he grew older he showed signs of unusual intelligence, learned to read and write, and eventually left the mountains to study at the *madrasah* (medieval college) in the city.

Just before he left the house, his mother wrapped his shepherd's cloak — *kapanak*[2] — in a cloth and gave it to him, saying, 'Take this with you and keep it safe, to remind you always who you are and where you are from.' She then murmured prayers of protection in his ears and, with tears in her eyes, she sent him on his way.

Naseem was sad to leave his home and his loving parents, but he knew that he had to pursue his own destiny. As soon as he arrived in the city he went straight to the *madrasah* and became a student. He was given a cell to live in and a small stipend for basic necessities. At first he felt homesick and lonely, but he knew there was no going back and gradually he made friends with other students and got accustomed to his new circumstances.

He worked diligently and mastered the curriculum, and after a few years he was ready to enter the world. His masters were impressed with his exceptional abilities and recommended him for a post in the King's administration, where he quickly rose in rank, his progress smoothed by his wit, charm and readiness to help others. In the end he became the Grand Vizir and the bosom friend of Soltan Mahmoud, the Padishah of Persia, and that is where our story begins.

In the meantime Naseem's parents had grown old. You know that when we want to express our thanks to someone who has been kind to us we say, 'May God make your end good', for it is in old age that poverty and ill-health are hardest to bear. Well, Naseem's parents' end was made comfortable and dignified by their dutiful and loving son, and they died content. Naseem distributed alms on their behalf and remembered them every day of his life in his prayers.

As for Soltan Mahmoud, well, he was so impressed by Naseem's goodness and competence that he grew more and more fond of him. He expressed his gratitude and affection by lavishing presents on him — land and gems and horses and camels, all of the highest quality — and even built him a palace next to his own so that they could be constantly near one another.

Now every day Naseem got up at dawn, said his prayers, and went into a secret closet in his bedroom, hidden behind a thick curtain, where he opened a safe, took out his shepherd's *kapanak*, put it on and looked at himself in the mirror. 'Don't forget who you are and where you are from,' he murmured, just as his mother had told him to do the day he had left their village all those years ago. This little ritual protected him from pride and arrogance, from thinking that his good fortune was entirely due to himself and not to the Grace of God.

One morning Soltan Mahmoud woke up very early and could not go back to sleep. He got up and went to his Grand Vizir's house to surprise him with his visit. The sky was pearly and the sun had not yet appeared on the horizon. All was quiet in Naseem's Palace, save for the twitter of birds waking up in the garden.

He found Naseem's room and looked through the window. He found him at prayer and waited for him to finish. Then he saw him pull aside a thick curtain, open the door of a closet and disappear inside. After a while he emerged, closed the hidden door and pulled back the curtain. He performed his dawn prayers and proceeded to put on his courtly clothes. Soltan Mahmoud was puzzled and decided not to show himself. He tiptoed back to his own room and waited for his Vizir to appear for his morning audience.

The next day Soltan Mahmoud got up at dawn and walked quietly to Naseem's house where he again witnessed the same ritual: his Grand Vizir saying his prayers, disappearing into the closet, emerging after a while and so on. After a few days the King wondered what on earth was in the closet: could it be a human being, an animal, a treasure of some sort Naseem was hiding? And how could he find out?

Now Naseem had a beautiful and clever daughter called Mahbanou ('Lady Moon') who was the lady-in-waiting and companion to the King's own daughter. Mahmoud summoned her and asked her to find out what her father did every morning in that closet and report back to him.

Mahbanou was in a quandary — she could not disobey the Soltan and she did not wish to betray her father's secret. She decided to find out for herself, and if there was anything incriminating, she would warn her father.

One day she crept into her father's room without being noticed by anyone, found the key to the closet and had a duplicate made. At night she let herself into the closet before her father came to his room and hid behind a stack of carpets and cushions. At dawn her father came into the closet and she witnessed him go through his little ritual: he took out the *kapanak* from a safe and put it on, looked at himself in the mirror and said, 'Don't forget who you are and where you are from.' Then he took it off, wrapped it in its cloth and put it back in the safe, and went out.

Mahbanou sighed with relief: not only was there nothing incriminating in his father's behaviour, but on the contrary it showed his humility and the grandeur of his soul. She gladly reported everything she had seen to Soltan Mahmoud. He was happy and thanked God for providing him with a vizir who was not only competent and learned but also godly and modest, and he loved Naseem even more. Indeed he became so attached to Naseem that he could not be parted from him for a single moment. Even when he was tired, he did not let his friend go; instead he lay his head on his lap and went to sleep.

One day Soltan Mahmoud gave a great banquet to welcome the Ambassador of the Khan of China. It was a magnificent occasion, the Padishah showing his power and wealth by the splendour of his Palace and the lavishness of his hospitality. Thousands of candles illuminated the halls and reception rooms, magnified tenfold by their reflection in the mirrors and crystal chandeliers; courtiers in sumptuous attires sat in a large circle around the King's golden throne, with the Khan's Ambassador placed beside him on his right, while delectable food and drink were served by servants and cup-bearers — *saqis.* The Ambassador was suitably impressed, the reception was deemed a triumph, and afterwards Soltan Mahmoud thanked Naseem for the success of the evening and he retired for the night.

The next evening it was the Grand Vizir's turn to give hospitality to the Chinese Ambassador. The King was attending and Naseem arranged a reception worthy of His Majesty. Bedecked with flowers and lit with thousands of torches and candles, his Palace shone in the night like a fairyland. The food was as varied as it was plentiful, wine and sherbet flowed, musicians played and dancers danced, and the guests stayed until dawn, reluctant to let such a feast come to an end. To tell the truth — they whispered —

Naseem's reception had surpassed that of the King the night before in grandeur and munificence.

When the guests had departed, Naseem retired to his bedchamber, satisfied that the evening had been a great success. As he was about to undress, he caught a glimpse of himself in the mirror, tall and imperious in full courtly regalia, and he had a shock, as if he had seen a stranger.

'Could this grand seigneur really be me, Naseem, the poor shepherd boy?' he said to himself. 'What a long way I have come! And what a lofty station I have reached, indispensable to my Sovereign and beloved by the people, unequalled in wealth and power, even outshining the King in my hospitality! Surely I am blessed.' His heart filled with pride and a smile of self-satisfaction hovered on his lips. He undressed and went to bed happy, and slept soundly.

A few months passed. One afternoon Soltan Mahmoud and Naseem went for a walk in the Palace gardens to take some fresh air and discuss the affairs of state. It was late autumn, the trees were denuded and the garden looked forlorn in the gathering dusk, and the King felt a twinge of melancholy. In those days it was not like now when you have flowers all year round, grown in greenhouses and sold in shops; nature took its course and people followed the rhythm of the seasons. There were of course some flowers in winter, like the winter jasmine, but certainly no roses, which is the queen of flowers and which everyone loves above all else.

Anyway, suddenly the King saw a single bloom high up on a wall, a magnificent white rose shining in the gloom like a star, as if it had survived by some miracle to lift the King's spirits. He longed to have it, but it was too high to reach and Naseem immediately offered his shoulders to him to climb on. Mahmoud refused, asking Naseem to climb on his shoulders instead.

There followed a good deal of courtesy exchanges — *taarof*[3] — Naseem offering his shoulders to the King and he graciously refusing and presenting his own to Naseem. Finally the Vizir gave in and stood on Soltan Mahmoud's shoulders, stretched out his arm and picked the rose. As he was getting down, once again he felt astonished. 'Is it I, the poor shepherd boy, standing on the shoulders of the Shahanshah, the most powerful man in the world?' he said to himself, and once again his heart filled with pride.

A few days later Soltan Mahmoud was having a nap in his room; as usual his head was resting on Naseem's knees. Suddenly a ravishing young man, dressed in a flowing white robe, appeared in the room. This was the inner sanctum of the King and no one had access to it; there were dozens of guards and servants at every step to stop any trespasser, and Naseem was astonished that this young man had managed to get past them all.

'Who are you?' he asked harshly. 'And what do you want?'

'I am your Luck,' the intruder smiled, 'and I have come to tell you that I am going to sleep.[4] I have been behind you ever since you left your village, but now I'm leaving you and going to sleep.'

Naseem got angry at such impertinence and drew his dagger to threaten the young man, but he vanished.

At that very moment Soltan Mahmoud woke up and saw Naseem with his dagger drawn. Since there was no one else in the room he asked for an explanation. Naseem seemed agitated. All he would say was: 'He has gone to sleep, but I can't tell.' No matter how much the King insisted, Naseem would say no more, and Mahmoud was forced to conclude that his trusted and beloved Grand Vizir intended to assassinate him and take his place.

Naseem was taken to the dungeons and tortured. They wanted him to confess his evil plot and denounce his accomplices, but he would say nothing, only repeating, 'He has gone to sleep and I can't tell.'

Eventually he was condemned to death. The news of his plight spread through the realm. People could not believe that their good Vizir was capable of such treachery — surely there was some misunderstanding? — and they felt sorry for him.

On the day he was to be executed, Naseem was led to the main square of the city where a gibbet had been erected and a huge crowd had gathered.

Meanwhile there were arguments and intrigues at the Court. Some of those who were envious of Naseem's position were secretly glad at his downfall, but most of the courtiers felt sad for him and pleaded for him. At first Mahmoud was angry and would not listen to them, but gradually he calmed down and softened. He agreed to spare Naseem's life, condemning him instead to permanent exile. He was not to be seen within five hundred miles of the capital, failing which he would be put to death at once.

A messenger was dispatched to the square and he arrived in the nick of time. Just as the executioner was fastening the rope around Naseem's neck, he announced the Soltan's decree. The crowd was jubilant. 'Long live the Padishah!' they cried. 'Long live the Grand Vizir!'

Stripped of his worldly possession and separated from his family, Naseem was taken to the gates of the city and thrown out. Once again he was wearing his shepherd's cloak, his old *kapanak*; ahead of him stretched a long road leading to oblivion. He walked all day and at night he slept in caves; he ate whatever he could find by way of roots and berries, and he drank only when he happened on a spring. Sometimes in villages he helped a shepherd or lent a hand to a farmer, and was given food and shelter in recompense.

After several months crossing deserts and mountains, he reached the edge of the city of Kashan, where he was given shelter by the miller. As it happened the miller's assistant had died, and Naseem took his place. He woke every day at dawn and worked until dusk, and at night he slept on a raised platform amid the sacks of grain and flour. His boss was a kind man and grew fond of him, and Naseem was content.

Seven years passed. Soltan Mahmoud often thought of Naseem and missed him. He was sad that such a great bond as theirs had been broken, but what else could he have done? He wondered where Naseem had vanished to, or indeed whether he was still alive. Some of the older and wiser courtiers talked to the King, saying that Naseem had no ill intentions, that perhaps he had momentarily lost his mind, for surely no servant of the King was more honest and loyal than he was. In this way they gradually prepared the King for a pardon.

One night Naseem was going to bed, exhausted and weary, when suddenly the ravishing young man in a white robe, who had first appeared before him in the Soltan's room seven years earlier, was standing there before him.

'Do you remember me?' he smiled. 'I'm your Luck, and I've come to tell you that I've now woken up again.'

Naseem asked him why he had decided to go to sleep and ruin his life in the first place.

The young man answered, 'Twice you allowed pride to fill your heart, once after the banquet you gave for the envoy of the Khan of China, and again when you climbed on the King's shoulders in the garden to pick the white rose. You thought your good fortune was due to your own cleverness and not to the Grace of God. You forgot that there are others as able as you are but less lucky. So I had to teach you a lesson before you lost your head completely, for the good of your own soul. You have done well since then and your heart has become pure again, so I've come back to tell you that I've woken up now. Once again I will be behind you wherever you go.' Saying this, and before Naseem had time to ask what he should do now that his Luck was awake, the young man vanished.

That very night Soltan Mahmoud had a dream: he saw a beautiful young man clad in a white robe appear in his room, and he said to him, 'Oh King of Persia! King of Kings! You had a perfect Grand Vizir, wise, able, loyal, and you got rid of him out of suspicion and pride. You may be a great conqueror, but surely you have no sense. Send for him while you still have time, for grave dangers lie ahead and no one except Naseem can avert them.' And before Mahmoud had time to ask who he was the young man vanished.

Mahmoud woke up. It was dawn. He thought his dream was surely a warning from the Occult World and he immediately ordered that messengers be dispatched all over the country to find Naseem and bring him back to the Court. Hundreds of couriers went and searched every village and town, but Naseem was nowhere to be found. They were about to give up in despair when someone discovered Naseem in the mill near Kashan and recognized him. He was taken back to the Court where Soltan Mahmoud received him graciously and reinstated him as the Grand Vizir.

The population was jubilant and flocked to the Palace in their thousands. 'Long live the Shahanshah!' they shouted. 'Long live Naseem!'

Soltan Mahmoud ordered the city to be illuminated and a public feast to be organized in every district. He ruled Persia for many more years in peace and prosperity, with Naseem's help overcoming the dangers that arose.

So you see, pride, arrogance and conceit can destroy a human being. However exalted your position, you must never forget that you are there by the Grace of God. You must never forget the poor and the unfortunate, lest your Luck decide to go to sleep like Naseem's, and you too become poor and unfortunate.

The Laughing Scarecrow

There was one and there was none/Except for God there was no one.

There was once an *âbed* (ascetic), who had dedicated his life to the worship of God and the obedience of His command- ments. He turned his back on the world and went to live in a cave in the mountains; he fasted all year round, and spent his days and nights praying and murmuring invocations and calling God's Names. Everyone in the neighbouring villages had heard of this *âbed* and respected his sincere piety and unworldliness.

Not that extreme asceticism is always a good thing, mind you. On the contrary, we must enjoy what God in His wisdom and mercy has provided for us and give thanks, as the Prophet and the saints and sages have enjoined us to do. But we must be moderate in our enjoyment of the fruits of creation, so there is enough for everybody.

Anyway, this *âbed* ate rarely and very little — only some bread and cheese that a shepherd or wayfarer gave him, asking for noth- ing in return except to be remembered in his prayers.

Time passed. It happened that one day nobody called in to give the *Âbed* some food. He waited patiently, trusting in God to provide for him — remembering that 'whosoever gives the teeth, gives the bread for them to chew', as the poet says. At night when he finished his prayers he went to bed on an empty stomach, trusting that the next morning someone would remember him and bring him at least a piece of rye bread. But no one came, and again he prayed all day and went to bed without supper. After a few days he began to feel the pangs of hunger, and when a week passed by with no food at all he was so famished that he could hardly murmur his invocations. His tummy ached and he felt giddy.

He decided to leave the cave and search for something, some fruit or berries or roots, to assuage his hunger. Perhaps he would meet a shepherd who would share his piece of bread with him.

All around his cave were bare mountains, but as he walked on he came to a green valley with a stream meandering through it, bordered with willows and poplars. He followed its course and presently the valley widened and a small village appeared, with orchards and fields.

'God be praised!' he exclaimed. 'I'm saved.'

Right before him a slope was covered with wild wheat; it was the height of the season and the golden ears of ripe corn swayed in the breeze. The Ascetic cut a few ears with his bare hands, sat on the bank of the stream in the shade of a willow tree, and began to separate the grains from the chaff and eat them avidly.

When he had eaten his fill, he lay down and had a little snooze, then he walked back to his cave, giving thanks to God for the wild corn and the sweet water. He prayed a long time and then lay down to sleep. But try as he might, he could not drop off. This time it was not the pangs of hunger that gnawed at him and kept him awake but his conscience: he wondered whose corn it was that he had taken and eaten. Perhaps it belonged to a widow whose livelihood depended on it? Or was it the only source of nourishment of some orphans? In which case he had committed a grave sin and God would surely punish him.

The next morning he walked to the valley and this time he went into the village. People were surprised to see him, and a good woman invited him to her cottage and offered him a bowl of warm fresh milk with some newly baked bread. In the course of conversation he found out that the wild wheat he had found on the hillside was indeed the only source of food of a widow with three fatherless children. He was deeply contrite to have eaten some of it, but what is done cannot be undone and he did not have a farthing or any possessions with which to compensate the widow for what he had taken from her. He thanked the good woman for her hospitality and left with a heavy heart.

Now it is said that we pay for our misdeeds and are rewarded for our good actions, either in this world or in the next, depending on God's judgement, for He is just and merciful. So as the *Âbed* walked back to his cave he began to pray and supplicate God, saying, 'Oh Lord! I know that I have done grievous wrong by taking from the poor widow's wheat, and therefore I have to be punished, but whatever the price of my sin let me pay for it here and now, in this world not in the next, so that when I reach my eternal abode I can face you cleansed and free.'

God evidently heard his pleas and granted his wish, for presently he was changed into a bullock. He found himself beside the stream and began to nibble at a tuft of grass.

As it happened there was a farmer nearby whose bullock had recently died of old age and he was desperate to acquire another one, for without one he could not plough his field and provide for his family. But he had no money with which to buy a bullock and he was in a quandary. Walking to his field and pondering the problem, he came upon a hefty bullock grazing by the stream. He wondered who it belonged to. It looked young and healthy, its jet black pelt glistening in the sun: it was just the animal he needed. He decided to find out its owner and perhaps come to an arrangement with him, buy it at a reasonable price and pay for it slowly in instalments. But try as he might, he could not find anyone who claimed the bullock or knew anything about it. He concluded that a tribe of nomads had passed by, that the bullock had strayed and that it had been left behind and forgotten. This was surely Providence coming to his aid, he thought, and he thanked God for His infinite compassion and took the bullock home.

A bullock's life is not an easy one. It is used for ploughing the fields, threshing the corn, transporting heavy loads and performing a variety of other chores on the farm, all for a little grass at the end of the day. In fact his fate is not much different from our own, I might add: for most of us work hard to earn our daily bread. But our bullock was content, for he knew that the change was only in his appearance, that inside he was still the same old *âbed* and that after this short life his soul would go to Heaven for eternity.

Several years passed. The bullock grew old and one day he died. The farmer sold its skin to the tanner, threw its carcass out into the wilderness for scavenging animals and birds, and kept its head to make a scarecrow. He stripped it, stuck the skull on a long stick, dressed it with some old clothes and a felt hat, and put it in the middle of his field to frighten off the birds and protect his crop. After a while he found another bullock which he bought at a fair price, and soon he forgot about his patient old workmate.

That summer the farmer's crop was exceptionally rich. He harvested and threshed it, and packed the grains in sacks ready to be taken to the market. By the time he had finished it was late, the sun had set and he was very tired. He left the sacks of grain in the field and went home. It was a bright, starry night; the countryside glowed, and you could find your way by the light of the stars.

Around midnight three thieves were walking past the field and they saw the sacks of grain, all packed and ready. What amazing luck!, they thought: they could take the whole lot with no fear of being seen by anyone.

Quickly each took one sack on his back and another in his arms and made to leave, when suddenly they heard loud laughter. They were so startled that they dropped the sacks; they were about to run away, but they looked around and they couldn't see anyone at all. The countryside was quiet and nothing moved.

They swore, picked up the sacks again and began to walk away, but the eerie laughter burst out again, this time even louder. Again they looked everywhere and saw nobody, not even the shadow of a ghost. When for the third time the laughter resounded and they looked about them, their jaws dropped in astonishment: it was the scarecrow guffawing, its teeth clucking and its empty black eye-sockets staring at them. They laughed with relief, saying it was the wind echoing in the skull and making the noise.

'What the hell are you laughing at, accursed animal, and scaring us out of our wits?' joked one of them.

To their utter amazement the scarecrow began to talk, saying, 'I was thinking about how I once stole a few ears of wild corn to assuage my hunger and for my sin I was turned into a bullock, made to toil for years and ended up as a skull perched on this stick, and I wondered what punishment God would mete out to you three for stealing the entire crop of a poor farmer, depriving him and his family of their livelihood.'

Hearing this, the three thieves felt ashamed, put down the sacks of grain, and went away. The fear of God's wrath entered their hearts by means of the *Âbed*'s skull, which shows by what roundabout ways God sometimes opens the eyes and hearts of His creatures.

The next day the farmer found his sacks of grain intact, took them to the market and sold them at a good price, unaware of how his livelihood had been saved. The three thieves decided to work for a living and keep to a straight and narrow path. And the scarecrow was discarded in due course and replaced by another one. But by then the *Âbed* was in Heaven, his tribulations long over.

The Good Young Man and the Heavenly Woman

There was one and there was none/Except for God there was no one.

Once upon a time there was a widow in Shiraz who had a son called Rashid. He was a charming and honest young man, loved and admired by everyone in the community. He was apprenticed to a herbalist in the Bazaar when he was fourteen, and after a few years, when he had learnt all there was to know about herbs and their medicinal properties, the herbalist made him his assistant and partner. It was a good profession, his boss was kind and he seemed happy. The herbalist's customers liked dealing with Rashid and often complimented him, saying how attractive and helpful he was and what a good husband he would make for some lucky young girl.

When Rashid was eighteen, his mother began to broach the subject of marriage; she would look for a suitable wife for him, she said, whenever he was ready. As a matter of fact she knew several young girls he could consider. But whoever she suggested, Rashid refused, saying, 'I don't want to get married unless I find an angel,

a woman who is a heavenly creature, with a pure soul.' When his
mother quizzed him about what he meant, he would say no more.
After she had found him several potential brides, all of them pretty
and modest, and he had rejected all of them, saying 'I'm waiting for
an angel', his mother began to despair and she gave up trying.
'Maybe one day he'll change his mind,' she said to herself.

Time passed. One Friday at noon, when mother and son were
making their ablutions for the midday prayer, there was a knock on
the door. Rashid's mother went and opened the door, and there
before her stood the most beautiful young woman she had ever
seen. She glowed like a lamp and lit up the air around her.

The mother was dazzled and it took her a while before she
could ask, 'Who are you and what is your wish?'

The young woman answered, 'I've come to see Rashid.'

The mother ran and told her son that a most ravishing girl was
at the door asking for him, and Rashid went to see who it was. As
soon as he set eyes on the young woman he knew she was the angel
he had been waiting for, that his dream had come true. He fell in
love with her 'not with one heart but with a hundred', as they say.
He blushed and lowered his eyes modestly. 'Welcome!' he said
softly and led her in.

The young woman stayed with Rashid and his mother, and
turned out to be as kind and intelligent as she was beautiful. Such
was the awe her beauty and dignity inspired that Rashid did not
dare ask her too many questions about herself, who she was and
where she came from, but she herself gradually volunteered the
information: her name was Pari-Rokh ('Fairy-Face' or 'Angel-
Face')[1] and she had come in answer to his prayers.

And indeed she did have angelic qualities — beauty, grace,
kindness, wisdom. Rashid was head over heels in love with her and
wanted to marry her. He proposed and she accepted him, saying, 'I
will marry you, but only on one condition.'

'What is it?' asked Rashid. 'I agree whatever it may be.'

Pari-Rokh said, 'The condition is that whatever I do, you neither question my reason nor blame me. One word of reproach or admonition and I shall be gone forever.'

Rashid accepted with alacrity, secure that such an angel would always be beyond reproach and that her behaviour would always be perfect.

And so they married and were blissfully happy. Within a year Pari-Rokh produced a baby, a little girl as pretty and angelic as her mother, but after thirteen days Pari-Rokh took her baby to the roof and threw it down; the baby's skull cracked and she died instantly. Rashid was horrified, but he remembered their pact — that whatever his wife did he would not ask any question or utter any reproach — and he said nothing. But he was heartbroken at the loss of his baby girl.

After a while his wife became pregnant again and this time gave birth to a perfect little boy. Rashid was overjoyed; he cuddled and kissed the boy tenderly. Ten days later, when the family were sitting by the fire about to have dinner, Pari-Rokh suddenly picked up the sleeping baby and threw it in the fire. Rashid was desperate and rushed to rescue the baby, but it was too late. The baby was dead.

Pari-Rokh reminded him of their pact and he said nothing. He trusted his wife, but this was beyond his comprehension, especially since Pari-Rokh was a most loving, caring mother.

Another year passed and this time Pari-Rokh gave birth to another little girl, but after three days she drowned it in the pool. Rashid was beside himself with grief, but he could say nothing, for fear of losing his wife.

In the meantime Rashid's mother had grown old and one day she fell ill. Pari-Rokh nursed her with care and affection, but the old woman's time was up and she died. On the day of the funeral, all the neighbours gathered and, as the coffin was being carried out of the house, the men chanting '*Allah-o-Akbar*' (God is Great) and the women wailing, Pari-Rokh climbed on the roof and started laughing. She laughed and laughed, as if she were watching a hilariously funny scene, until the funeral cortege disappeared down the street. Everybody was astonished and embarrassed at her behaviour. It was usual for a daughter-in-law to weep and wail if she lost her mother-in-law. Even if the mother had been cruel and bossy, the daughter-in-law used to fake some token tears, to please her husband and his family. But Pari-Rokh had always got on with her mother-in-law and showed her affection and the respect due to old age, so why was she laughing as if with joy at her death and embarrassing her husband in front of neighbours and acquaintances?

That evening Rashid could no longer contain his anger and frustration, and he said to his wife, 'Come and sit down, I have something to ask you.'

Pari-Rokh knew what was on his mind and she gently warned him, 'Remember, we made a pact that you would never question or blame me for anything I did. So please don't say anything.'

Rashid was too angry and distressed to heed her warning and he insisted on an explanation. 'You killed our babies,' he said, 'one after another, all three of them, and I held my tongue. Now you laugh at my mother's funeral. I must know the reason for all this.'

Pari-Rokh had no choice but to tell him. 'I threw down our first-born from the roof thirteen days after she was born,' she said, 'because I knew she was going to die at the age of thirteen by falling from a height, and I thought the pain of losing her at that age would be harder to bear than if she died at thirteen days. Similarly our son, the second baby, was going to die at the age of seven by falling into a furnace and I thought it was better for him to die aged seven days than seven years. As for the third baby, she was going to drown at the age of three, and I preferred to spare her and us by letting her drown straightaway, when she was only three days old.

'Now as for your mother: she lived seventy years, and she was so mean and tight-fisted that she never gave anything to anybody. She saved her money in a pot which she hid in the closet behind some boxes where you can find it, instead of enjoying it and giving charity while she was alive. Only once in all her years did she manage to bring herself to part with anything: an old sheet which she gave to a poor woman who needed some cloth and could not afford to buy any. Now that she is dead she can take with her none of the money and gold she has accumulated; all she can take is the shroud in which her body was wrapped, just like the white sheet she gave to the poor old woman years ago. It was reflecting on this that made me laugh aloud. Now you know the reasons for all that I did.'

Having finished her say, and before Rashid could utter a word of apology for breaking their agreement, Pari-Rokh disappeared.

Rashid was inconsolable at her loss. God had granted him his heart's desire, he had prayed for an angel and He had sent him one, but he had doubted her goodness and wisdom, and now she was gone. This story illustrates what is said in the Holy Book, that things will happen to us which we don't like, but we must not question God's wisdom, for only He knows what is best for us.

The Thorn-Seller
and the Bird of Paradise

There was one and there was none/Except for God there was no one.

There was once an old *khar-kan* who lived with his wife in a green valley tucked away in the folds of the Alborz mountains. The valley was like a long patchwork of cornfields and meadows and pastures and orchards, with the silver thread of a stream running through it, and all around row upon row of arid hills rising higher and higher until the last ridges were lost in clouds. Nothing grew on the hills except dry, colourless scrub and thorn bushes with shallow roots and tangled spikes that could tear your skin if you were not careful. The villagers cultivated their pieces of land, husbanded their animals and sold their produce in the market. The only man who had no land and no flocks was the *khar-kan*, so he made a meagre living from digging up the thorn and scrub which covered the surrounding hills and selling it to the villagers for fire wood. Thorn bush is particularly good for baking bread in *tanours*, as it blazes quickly and produces a lot of heat, and after the bread is baked you can put your pot of soup on the embers to cook slowly for your dinner.

Every morning the thorn-seller got up at dawn, said his prayers, ate a piece of bread and set off for the hills. He dug and dug until he had lots of thorn bushes; then he gathered them into a huge bundle, loaded them on to his back and returned to the village to sell them from door to door. When he had finished, he went back to the hills to collect some more. Some times he collected two or three loads a day and sometimes only one, depending how far he had to go. Meanwhile his wife sat at her loom weaving cloth, which she sold to the draper to supplement their income. At sundown her husband came back, they had their evening meal and went to bed. It was a hard life, but they were content and gave thanks to God for providing them with a living by covering the hills with thorn and scrub.

One day the *khar-kan* went a long way away from his village into the mountains, making his way around several hills, and suddenly he came across a fountain, a trickle of water emerging from under the rocks and pouring into a small, shallow pool. Beside it rose a single tree, a huge, wild willow casting its shadow over the crystal-clear water. It was midday, the sun was high, and he was hungry and thirsty. He cupped his hands and drank from the delicious cold water; then he splashed some over his head and face, and sat down in the shade of the willow tree to rest and have some food. He opened the bundle of bread and cheese which his wife always prepared for him, and began to eat, happy to have found such a pleasant spot in the middle of the wilderness.

Suddenly he heard the sweet trill of a bird. It was unlike any birdsong he had ever heard, more mellifluous and delightful than a nightingale's. He looked up to see what kind of bird it was that made such an enchanting sound, and there among the higher branches was a golden cage and in it a beautiful bird such as he had never seen before, with feathers all the colours of the rainbow and an emerald-green beak. There was water in the cage, and seeds, but no one anywhere nearby.

As he was looking up in amazement, the bird began to sing again, as if for his benefit, its black-button eyes fixed on him. The thorn-seller was enchanted, but there was no way he could reach the cage and take it home. He wondered who had hung the bird up there, so high among the branches that no predators, no wild cats or snakes, could harm it. Besides, who could possibly live there, miles from any human habitation, in the midst of stark, rocky mountains and scrubland? It was all an enchanting mystery.

It occurred to him that if God provided shelter, food and water for this small beautiful bird in this vast, harsh wilderness, surely He could provide for him and his wife as well without him having to break his back digging up thorns all day long. He had worked hard all his life, and now that he was getting old and tired he longed to stop striving and spend the few years he had left in peace and contemplation. Without a doubt this was what the bird was trying to tell him with its song. The idea cheered him up no end; he went back to the village and sold his load of thorn, but instead of going back to the hills to collect some more, he went home.

His wife was surprised to see him arrive so early and asked him the reason. He told her about the strange bird and its magical song, adding that it was certainly a sign from the *Alam-e-Gheib* that he should stop struggling and instead trust Providence to provide for them. His wife thought that her poor old husband was exhausted and hallucinating, that he needed some rest. So they had their supper early and they went to bed.

In the morning she prepared his bundle of bread and cheese as usual, but to her surprise her husband said that he was not going to work. 'I told you last night that I'm tired of breaking my back for a pittance. I've worked enough and I'm getting old; from now on God will have to provide if He doesn't want us to starve.'

His wife tried to soothe him and reason with him, but he was adamant. 'Either God will take care of us or we shall perish,' he said, 'but I'm through with thorn-digging.'

Eventually his wife gave up arguing with him, and decided to go thorn-collecting in his place. She picked up his pick-axe and rope and set off for the hills, thinking that her poor husband had lost his mind and that from then on she would have to work for both of them, working as a *khar-kan* during the day and weaving at night.

She walked and walked through the rocky wilderness until she reached a hillside covered with thorn bushes, and there she began to dig. After a while her pick-axe hit something hard and she heard the jingle of metal. She cleared away the earth and found a huge iron chest, fastened with a padlock. She broke the padlock with her pick-axe and lifted the lid, and lo! the chest was brim-full of gold sovereigns, dazzling like the midday sun. She nearly fainted with astonishment. 'God be praised!' she exclaimed and she put her hand down into the chest. Beneath the coins she found jewellery worthy of the Queen of Sheba: strings of pearls as large as pigeon eggs, rings and bracelets and pendants, all made of diamonds, sapphires, emeralds and rubies of various sizes and shapes. Wondering if she was dreaming, she rubbed her eyes, picked up a fistful of gold coins and let them cascade on to the heap. She tried a diamond ring — it fitted perfectly. Oh yes, it was all real.

The chest was far too big and heavy for her to shift, so she covered it with earth, marked the spot with some rocks and dashed home to tell her husband. 'Come with me,' she said to him. 'You were right, the magic bird was a sign — I've found buried treasure.' And she told him how she had discovered the chest and what was in it.

But even the two of them could not lift the chest; they needed another strong pair of arms and a hefty mule to carry the treasure home. Who could they trust with the secret? There were thieves and ruffians in the Bazaar who, if they heard about it, would immediately claim and appropriate the chest and give them nothing. What were they to do?

Now they had a neighbour called Mashti Saleh[1] who was a shopkeeper in the village *Bazaarcheh* (little bazaar) selling household goods, and they believed him to be an honest man. They called him in, told him the story of the treasure trove and asked him to help them dig up the chest and carry it home on his mule, in exchange for half the contents.

It couldn't be a fairer deal, and Mashti Saleh accepted it with alacrity. Without further ado he fetched his mule and the three of them went back to the hillside, found the spot and dug out the chest. It was indeed too heavy to lift, but they managed to haul it on to the back of the mule and they headed back home. They were so elated that they could almost fly; the shopkeeper prodded his mule to go faster and the thorn-seller was overjoyed that their tribulations were at an end.

As they approached the village and the safety of home, the Devil got into Mashti Saleh's mind and he was suddenly gripped by greed. He could not bear the thought of parting with half the treasure; he wanted to keep the whole lot for himself. He forgot his promise and wondered how he could best deceive his neighbours.

'My house is bigger than yours,' he told them. 'We can take the chest there, empty the contents on the floor and divide it equitably.'

They agreed. Once inside the house, Mashti Saleh said that it was late and he was feeling tired: would they mind leaving the matter until the next morning? The *khar-kan*'s wife was reluctant, but her husband agreed and they went home.

They could hardly sleep with excitement, saying that by the Grace of God all their worries were over, and they began making plans for the future. They were now rich enough to make the pilgrimage to Mecca and become *hajis*, and afterwards they would go to Meshed and visit the shrine of Imam Reza, and then ... and then ... Oh there was no end to their dreams. Above all their old age would be free from poverty and shame.

At dawn they got up and went to their neighbour's house to share the treasure. Mashti Saleh opened the door looking sleepy and surprised to see them, and asked what they wanted.

'We've come to share the treasure,' they said.

'What treasure? What are you talking about?' he retorted, feigning ignorance. 'Are you mad? Waking people up at the crack of dawn talking nonsense about hidden treasure. Go away and don't bother me any more.'

You can imagine how the poor *khar-kan* and his wife felt. They pleaded and begged and appealed to his pity, but Mashti Saleh would not be moved. When the Devil puts greed into a heart, pity goes out of it and an honest shopkeeper turns into a ruthless scoundrel. Mashti Saleh told them they were either crazy or wicked, trying to extort money out of him, and finally he kicked them away and banged the door, cursing and threatening to call the village headman and have them jailed.

The *khar-kan* and his wife went home in despair. Who would believe them if they told their story? Mashti Saleh was a respectable shopkeeper and people would naturally accept his word rather than theirs. Everyone would laugh at their fantastic fairytale, and they might even be thrown into a lunatic asylum. No, it was better to accept defeat and tell no one. The thorn-seller's wife sat in a corner and wept bitterly, calling on God, the Prophet and the Imams to come to their rescue and soften the heart of their neighbour.

In those days country huts were built with mud and straw and had flat roofs. There was usually a hole in the roof above the storage place, which was covered with a heavy stone to stop rain and snow pouring through it. This was because in summer people spread fruit and herbs and vegetables on their roofs to dry in the sun. Afterwards they poured all this down into sacks on the ground, and stored it away for the winter.

Well, seeing his wife heartbroken, weeping and lamenting, the *khar-kan* felt very sorry for her; her grief touched him more than the loss of the treasure, but what could he do? He had almost resigned himself to the thought of having to go back to thorn-selling when he remembered the fountain in the wilderness, the willow tree, the magical bird, the bird's heavenly song and keen black eyes, and he felt reassured that somehow God would provide. He tried to console his wife and shore up her faith in Providence.

'Don't worry,' he told her. 'If it is our fate to be poor forever, we shall have to manage as we did before, but if it's God's will that our circumstances change for the better, He can drop a new treasure down through that hole', and he pointed to the hole in the roof.

Now what about the wicked Mashti Saleh, the respectable shopkeeper, who had made the pilgrimage to Meshed and vowed to be always an honest dealer? That night he could not sleep for joy — why, he was rich beyond his wildest dreams! He would sell up his business and travel to Hindustan, buy himself a palace, marry a princess and live like a maharaja. He would have peacocks in his gardens and parrots in his trees; he would ride elephants and shoot tigers; he would be surrounded by courtiers and bards and musicians and dancers; he would have a Harem full of women as beautiful as *houris*. What a charmed life!

He got up and went into his back-room closet where he had hidden the chest of gold and jewellery, and opened it to feast his eyes on the dazzling sovereigns. But as soon as he removed the padlock and lifted the lid, he jumped back in horror and uttered a scream: the chest was full of snakes and spiders and scorpions of all sizes and colours, and they were crawling out into his house. He quickly banged the lid shut and put on the padlock. His golden dreams turned into ashes instantly, and he cursed the thorn-seller and his wife, for he was sure they had put a spell on the treasure to turn it into poisonous reptiles. He vowed he would teach them a lesson!

He pulled the chest out, which was surprisingly light without its gold and jewels, carried it to his own roof, dragged it across to the *khar-kan's* roof, pushed back the stone that covered the hole, opened the lid and began to empty the reptiles down the hole.

'I hope you'll both be bitten by the first adder and die instantly!' he muttered to himself.

But lo! as the snakes and scorpions and spiders began dropping down the opening they all turned into gold coins.

'Good Lord!' he exclaimed. 'What am I doing? I must have been feverish and hallucinating in the store-room, seeing creepy-crawlies instead of gold.'

Luckily the chest was still over half full, so he quickly slammed the lid and dragged the chest back to his own house.

Meanwhile the *khar-kan* and his wife saw the stone being lifted from the hole in the roof and a cascade of gold sovereigns pouring down into the room.

'Didn't I tell you,' said the thorn-seller to his wife, 'that if God wishes us to have treasure He can drop it down through the hole above our heads?' They picked up the sovereigns and put them in a bag, relieved and happy.

Mashti Saleh went back to bed, but try as he might he could not go to sleep, wondering how he could have mistaken his beloved treasure for deadly poisonous creatures. He got up, went into his closet and opened the chest to reassure himself. Once more, as soon as the lid was lifted, spiders, snakes and scorpions began to crawl out. He quickly shut the lid again, pulled the chest back up on to the roof, dragged it across to his neighbour's roof and began emptying it down the hole. Again the creepy-crawlies turned instantly into gold coins and jewellery. He slammed the lid shut and dragged the chest back to his own house.

Throughout the night every time he opened the chest, he found it full of spiders and adders and scorpions, and as soon as he began dropping them down into his neighbour's house they metamorphosed into gold coins and gems.

Finally there was only one gold sovereign left in the chest, but that too became a huge cobra when he tried to pick it up. This time he let the lethal creature carefully out of the chest into a sack, fastened the top with a piece of string, took it up to the roof and dropped it through the thorn-seller's roof-hole, saying, 'This one is in a bag and I hope it will kill you both when you open it!'

The *khar-kan's* wife opened the sack and in it found the string of pearls that had so dazzled her when she first found the treasure.

So you see, but for his greed the shopkeeper would have kept half the treasure, enough to realize all his dreams. Instead he lost the lot and stayed in his village with his little shop for the rest of his life, while the *khar-kan* and his wife went on pilgrimage to Mecca and became *hajis*. On their return to Persia they settled in Meshed near the shrine of Imam Reza and became generous benefactors to the community. They were loved and respected by everyone, and lived happily to a great age.

Soltan Mahmoud
and the Band of Robbers

There was one and there was none/Except for God there was no one.

Once upon a time there was a king of Persia called Soltan Mahmoud.[1] He had started life as the chief of some Turkic tribes in Central Asia and ended up conquering Persia and becoming Padishah. A wild, rough warrior who had lived on horseback in the middle of the steppes, he settled down and became a superb king. He built a palace in his capital Ghazneh where he set up a vast court, with thousands of courtiers and servants, to which he invited poets and savants from all over the empire and beyond.

They say that at the height of his power Soltan Mahmoud had four hundred poets at his Court, living and working under his munificent patronage, and writing in praise of his valour and generosity. It was Soltan Mahmoud who commissioned Firdowsi to write the *Shahnameh* (*The Book of Kings*). This took the poet thirty years — but that's another story.

Anyway, Soltan Mahmoud was in the habit of roaming the streets of his capital at night incognito, alone or with his Vizir, disguised as an ordinary man in modest clothes, to see for himself if all was well in his kingdom. He would go to taverns and mix with all kinds of people, humble or rich, and engage them in conversation or listen to their talk, to find out what they thought of him and his rule, his vizirs and counsellors, whether they were content or rebellious, peaceful or plotting against him. He compared what he heard with the reports of his courtiers and spies, testing their honesty and sincerity. This was his way of keeping in touch with his people directly and not relying only on flatterers and time-servers who might lie to him out of self-interest. Late at night when everybody dispersed and went home, he too made his way back to his Palace and went to bed. The next day he would deal with the grievances and criticisms he had heard. This kept his vizirs and counsellors on their toes and he reigned in peace.

One night Soltan Mahmoud was walking back to his Palace in the small hours when he came upon a band of robbers. The streets were dark and empty, and there was not a soul to come to his rescue if he were attacked. As it turned out the thieves were not after a fight, but they asked who he was and what he was doing in the pitch dark at such an ungodly hour. The Soltan replied that he was one of them, a burglar and thief looking for an opportunity, and he asked if he could join their band.

The thieves laughed at his cheek and they told him that not everybody could be a robber of their calibre. They weren't just petty thieves preying on innocent citizens but real professionals after bigger game, and each of them had some exceptional gift which guaranteed the success of their enterprise. They would take him on only if he too had a useful talent.

'So what is your ability?' they asked.

Mahmoud thought for a moment and replied, 'You tell me about yours first, and then I'll let you know mine.' They agreed.

The first thief said, 'My talent lies in my ears: when I hear a dog bark miles away I can understand what he is saying and so I can prepare against unforeseen events. If the animal says it is going to rain I can take shelter and if he foretells drought I can make provisions.'

This was indeed remarkable and Mahmoud could not claim to have the same ability. He turned to the second thief and asked him about his exceptional gift.

'My skill resides in my eyes,' he replied. 'Whoever I see in the darkness of night, I can recognize in broad daylight the next day. For example if a pickpocket attacks me at night and runs off with my purse and I come across him the following morning in the Bazaar, I recognize him and tackle him to get it back.'

Mahmoud conceded that this quality was most unusual too.

Then it was the turn of the third. 'My strength is in my arms,' he said. 'I can dig the ground fast and deep, no matter how hard it may be, to reach whatever treasure it holds.'

'God be praised!' exclaimed the Soltan. 'A very useful ability.'

Next he turned to the fourth man. 'My gift is my nose,' said the thief. 'The earth has no secret for me; I can smell the earth and know at once if gold or precious stones are buried underneath, just as a lover can recognize the smell of his beloved from a discarded handkerchief, just as Majnoun can smell the ground and know that Leyly has walked on it.'[2]

Finally the last of the band said that his talent was in his hands: 'I can throw a lasso, or a rope or a hook, higher than any human being, and so scale any wall no matter how high.'

When the robbers had finished describing their expertise, they asked Mahmoud what he could contribute to the group.

Mahmoud said, 'My special quality is in my beard, for with it I can save a man's life. For example when a bandit has been caught and condemned to be hanged, I can shake my beard and have him reprieved immediately.'

The robbers couldn't believe such a thing was possible, but Mahmoud assured them that he was telling the truth and would prove it to them when the time came. At this they bowed before him, saying that his talent was the most useful of all, for sooner or later one or all of them were bound to be caught and brought to justice; they would certainly be sent to the gallows, and their new friend could save them by shaking his beard. They told Mahmoud that, in view of his life-saving skill, he would be their commander.

So the five friends began to walk together and look for an opportunity to make a raid. Presently the one who had acute hearing stopped and listened.

'I hear a dog barking outside the city gates,' he said. 'And he is saying that the Soltan is among us.'

This was clearly nonsense — how could the King be among a band of robbers when he was surely sound asleep in his Palace? They laughed heartily and said that for once their colleague's ears were letting him down.

After a while they came to a hill and the one who had a sharp nose said to them, 'Here a widow has buried her savings.' They were honourable thieves and didn't want to rob a poor woman, so they went on their way.

Finally they reached the King's Palace, surrounded by high walls. Here the partner whose talent was for throwing lassoes came into his own. He made a large noose at the end of a long, thick rope and threw it high up the wall; it caught the tip of the battlements and one by one they pulled themselves up and slid down the far side.

Presently the man who had a sharp nose smelled the ground and found the location of the Soltan's treasure-house. Next the partner with mighty arms and steely claws dug the earth away and revealed a trap door with a huge padlock which he broke like a wafer. Under the trap door they found a steep narrow staircase going down into the bowels of the earth. One by one they went down until they reached the bottom and found a dark tunnel. They groped their way along and arrived at an iron door as large and thick as the portal of the Grand Mosque. The man with strong arms managed to push it open and lo! there in front of them was the Padishah's treasury — a vast room full of coffers from floor to ceiling, overflowing with gold coins and precious stones. The man with the acute nose smelled the air and said that they were exactly under the Soltan's very bed-chamber, where he was doubtless sound asleep, unaware that his treasury was being robbed.

Once the robbers got over their astonishment, they quickly filled their bags with gold and made their way back to the surface and out of the Palace. Mahmoud followed them to their home, which was an old ruined *caravanserai* outside the city gates. The place had a reputation for being haunted by jinns and evil spirits and no one ever ventured there, which was why the thieves had chosen it as their hideout. Tired, hungry and excited after their exertions, the robbers shared some bread and cheese with their new partner, gave him a straw mattress and lay down to sleep.

As soon as Mahmoud heard them all snoring he got up quietly and slipped away without a sound. The sky was turning grey and the cocks were beginning to crow, and Soltan Mahmoud hurried to get back to his Palace before anyone could recognize him. He let himself in through a secret door which no one knew about except himself and his trusted Vizir, and went straight to his bed-chamber to have some sleep, pondering what to do with the thieves.

Later that morning, when the Court assembled, the Soltan told them the story. A party of soldiers was dispatched to recover the gold, arrest the thieves and bring them to the Court to be judged and sentenced.

As soon as the thieves entered the audience room and saw the Soltan on his throne, the thief with exceptional vision said, 'That is the man who was with us last night! He witnessed all our deeds and heard all our secrets.' At this they realized that nothing could save them from certain death. The executioner stood near the throne, waiting for a sign from the Soltan to chop off their heads.

'Well, what do you have to say for yourselves?' asked the Padishah. 'What punishment should I give you?'

The thieves said they did not deny their guilt, but that they had only done their job as best they could, each using his particular skill. It was now the Soltan's turn to use his special ability — to shake his beard and save all their lives.

Mahmoud laughed. He had to accept the logic of their argument: he had told them that by shaking his beard he could save their lives, and they had made him their commander. He had no choice but to be magnanimous and pardon them. The robbers for their part repented and promised to give up their profession and find honest employment.

This story comes from Rumi's Masnavi, but neither Zahra nor I knew its provenance. Many years later, when I first read the whole book, I recognized it. She had taken the gist of the story and built her own more elaborate version, without the poet's philosophical extrapolations. Rumi's poem is a parable concerning human sinfulness and divine mercy. Of the thieves' skills only the 'eye that recognizes a king' is worthwhile, and to a lesser degree the ear that can understand the dog's warning, while the other qualities, being purely material, bring them only trouble and prove useless in the face of death.

The Fortune-Teller's Fortune

There was one and there was none/Except for God there was no one.

L ong ago in the city of Isfahan there lived a man called Hemmat. He was very poor, for he had no special skills, and although he worked every day of the year from dawn to dusk at whatever jobs he could find, taking the hardest tasks on building sites and shifting heavy loads in the Bazaar until he felt his back was breaking, he barely earned a living. Yet he never complained; on the contrary, he was always content and cheerful.

'How come?' you may ask. On account of his wife Sediqa, who was beautiful like the full moon in a cloudless sky. She had eyes of liquid olive, the slender body of a young cypress tree, alabaster skin and the grace of a gazelle. Every night when Hemmat came home the sight of his lovely wife banished his fatigue and weariness, and the sun shone in his heart. 'The stars in Heaven would fade in shame if they saw your face,' he told her and he considered himself the luckiest man on earth.

Time passed. Sediqa gave birth to a son and then a daughter, and it became even harder to make ends meet with what Hemmat managed to earn. They reached a point when Sediqa could not afford the two farthings she needed for her weekly visit to the *Hammam*. For a while she made do with heating some water and washing herself at home, but she felt dirty and ashamed when neighbours said that they had not seen her at the baths for a long time, and she complained to her husband.

Eventually he managed to find the money, and Sediqa took her bundle of clean clothes and towels and went to the *Hammam*. To her surprise it was closed. The attendant told her that the *Hammam* had been booked exclusively — for the King's Chief Fortune-Teller's wife and her maids. Sediqa begged the attendant to let her in, for she had come a long way and she was badly in need of a proper bath. 'I will sit in a dark corner so as not to be seen, and I will be as quick as I can, but please don't send me away,' she pleaded, and the attendant felt sorry for her and let her in.

Sediqa undressed quickly and went into the big, hot room, lit only by glass portholes in the ceiling and swirling with steam that was as dense as an autumn fog. She sat in a dark corner and began to pour hot water over herself; her skin drank up the liquid as avidly as a thirsty traveller in a desert, and her limbs relaxed in pleasure after months of deprivation.

Presently the door opened and the Chief Fortune-Teller's wife came in, her arms held by two young maids walking on either side of her while a third carried a round silver tray and a fourth a silver basin and a bowl. They placed the tray on the floor and sat the Chief Fortune-Teller's wife on it to protect her bottom from the heat of the tiles; then they filled the basin with hot and cold water at just the right temperature before pouring it over her shoulders. One woman began to rub her back, another combed her hair, yet another applied henna to her nails and toes.

There was no nail varnish in those days, so women used henna to colour not only their fingernails and toenails but also the palms of their hands and the soles of their feet: beside its cheerful colour, you see, henna has special properties which protect one from certain ailments, such as itchiness and stiff joints.

Anyway, sitting in the shadows, Sediqa was not noticed, but in the steamy twilight she saw that the Chief Fortune-Teller's wife was ugly and misshapen; her face was long and bony like that of a starved sheep, with tiny close-set eyes and bushy eyebrows and thin lips. Her skin was patchy and wrinkled, she had a hunched back and she was always ill-humoured, snarling and snapping at her women with the shrill voice of a wild cat.

Sediqa felt a pang of pain. 'Oh God!' she sighed. 'You've made me as lovely as a fairy and given me a face to vie with the Queen of the Night; you've given me a good nature and a happy disposition. And yet my husband can't afford two farthings for my bath, while this hideous scarecrow is covered with gold and treated like a queen. Is it fair?'

All the same, she thanked the Lord for her loving husband and two healthy children. Besides, who knows God's intentions? He has good reasons for everything, only we don't know about them, for we can't fathom His mystery. So Sediqa enjoyed her bath thoroughly, slipped out without being seen and went home.

In the evening her husband came home and when they sat down to their modest meal she told him about her visit to the baths and seeing the Chief Fortune-Teller's wife.

'Forget about going to work tomorrow and killing yourself digging the ground and shifting heavy loads,' she said. 'From now on you are going to be a *Rammal* — a fortune-teller and astrologer.'

Hemmat laughed, thinking his wife was joking, but she insisted that she was deadly serious, adding, 'Either you become a fortune-teller and make a decent living for us, or I will divorce you.'

Hemmat begged her to be reasonable. 'I know nothing about the art,' he said. 'Besides I don't have the instruments for it.'

'Never mind,' retorted Sediqa. 'You'll sell your pick-axe and shovel and back-pad, and that will provide enough money to buy some fortune-telling dice and an astrolabe and set yourself up as a friend and confidant of the constellations above. When a client comes to see you, all you have to do is to throw your dice on the board, look intensely at your astrolabe while you turn it around in your hand, and tell them that the position of the planets is favourable to the enterprise they have in mind, that Gemini and Capricorn are in such and such a spot in the firmament and that therefore the client is bound to succeed. Leave the rest to the Almighty, for He is merciful and compassionate.'

Hemmat hardly slept. But he could not bear the thought of losing his beautiful wife if he failed at the very least to try his luck. As soon as the Bride of the Heavens sank beneath the horizon and the sky turned pearly he got up and went to the Bazaar. He sold his pick-axe, shovel and back-pad, and with the money he bought the necessary equipment for his new profession. He wrapped a piece of cotton around his peasant felt hat and put on a cloak that made him look like a learned man or a Mullah, and went to the Mosque. He found a shaded corner in the forecourt where he could be seen by everyone who came in, spread out a cloth, laid out his instruments and waited for clients.

After a while he began to get anxious: what if no one came to consult him? How could he go home empty-handed? How would he feed his family? He cursed himself for listening to his wife.

Presently the servant of the richest merchant in the Bazaar, Haji Mortaza, approached him anxiously and said, 'A camel loaded with gold and silver belonging to my master has bolted. I have looked everywhere for it, but it has simply vanished. Perhaps the jinns have taken it or else robbers have seized it. It can't just have disappeared into thin air. All I know is that unless I find it safe and sound, my master will hang me. Please use your skill and tell me where the accursed animal can be found.'

Our fortune-teller didn't have a clue. 'Oh merciful God!' he thought. 'Please help me!' He shook his dice and threw them on the board. The cameleer held his breath, while Hemmat first looked intently at the squiggle where the dice had landed and then looked into the astrolabe, which was covered with engravings of Arabic words and numbers that looked to him for all the world like insects crawling.

After scratching his chin, he said with a smile of satisfaction, 'Aha! I can see where your camel is, but you must first pay me ten *dirhams*.'

The man paid up gladly. After putting the money in his pocket, our new fortune-teller told the servant what he should do. 'Take a fistful of chickpeas,' he said, 'drop them one by one on the ground as you walk, and follow them to wherever they roll. When the last chickpea stops, close your eyes and turn round three times. Then open your eyes and walk straight ahead, and you will see your camel.'

The rich merchant's servant thanked the fortune-teller profusely and ran to do as he was bidden, full of hope that his life might be saved after all. He bought a fistful of chickpeas from the bean-seller in the Bazaar and, starting from where the fortune-teller was sitting, he began to roll them along the ground one by one, following their course until the last pea rolled a few feet and stopped. He then closed his eyes, turned round three times, opened his eyes again and walked straight ahead. He walked on for a while until he had left the city and there was nothing before him but wilderness. There was not a blade of grass to be seen, let alone a camel; there was nothing but scrubs and stones, only scrub and stones.

He began to despair. 'May that fortune-teller roast in Hell,' he mused. 'He took my money and sent me on a wild goose chase.'

Just as he was about to give up the search, he came upon the ruins of an old fort, and lo and behold, there was his camel with its cargo of gold and silver, resting in the shade of a broken-down wall, quietly ruminating. You can imagine his relief. He took the camel's reins and with words of endearment he gently got him up on his feet and walked back with him to his master's house.

He then told Haji Mortaza all that had happened and how the cunning clairvoyant had seen the exact location of the wayward camel and guided him to it. His master was so pleased that he gave the servant a gold coin and praised his fortitude.

That evening Hemmat went home to his family full of joy; he was loaded with succulent kebabs and steaming rice and cream cakes for their dinner. In a few minutes he had made more money than in a month of back-breaking toil. 'Little wifey,' he said to Sediqa, 'you were right. It's not so bad to be a fortune-teller after all.'

The next day Hemmat went back to the Mosque before the dawn prayer, sat down in the same spot and took out his dice and spread his instruments before him. After a while he saw the rich merchant's servant arrive, accompanied by three men, and he told him that his master wished to see him.

Hemmat's heart sank. 'Oh merciful God!' he thought. 'What can he want from me? And what if I fail his tests? I don't know the first thing about astrology and the art of divination; it was only by Your Grace that I got it right yesterday, but what will happen now? I shall be exposed as a fraud and kicked out.'

However, he had no choice but to follow the servants to Haji Mortaza's house. And what a house! It was like a prince's palace, set in the midst of gardens, with pools and fountains and a stream, birds singing in the trees and doves cooing on the eaves. He was led to a sumptuous room where the Haji was reclining on a dais uphol-stered in Indian brocade, attended by flunkies.

'Are you the *Rammal* who found my camel and its precious load?' he asked, and Hemmat admitted that he was. 'Well, as from today you shall be my Chief Astrologer and *Rammal*, and work for me exclusively.' He then gave Hemmat a fistful of gold coins as advance payment, saying, 'You shall receive the same amount every month so you won't need to do any other work.'

Hemmat thanked his new master for the honour. 'May the protection of Your Excellency never leave me,' he said. 'May the Lord grant you long life and good health.'

He bowed and left. He went straight home and spread the gold before his wife. 'I will have the same every month!' he told her. His wife was dazzled at the sight of the gold, and asked him what had happened. Hemmat told her the story, concluding, 'From now on I'm the Chief Astrologer and Fortune-Teller of the richest mer-chant in town, and yet I know absolutely nothing about the stars and have no skill in fortune-telling. What shall I do when my new master puts me to the test? I shall be unmasked and flogged, and thrown into a dungeon or out of the province. You see in what a dangerous position you have put me?'

Sediqa replied, 'Don't worry. Trust the Lord, for He is merci-ful and compassionate.'

Thereafter our Chief Astrologer and Master Fortune-Teller went to the merchant's house every morning at dawn and returned home at sundown, ready each day to be consulted about the posi-tion of the stars or the likely outcome of an enterprise.

For a while nothing happened and his services were not re-quired, and he thanked God for His mercy. Then one night a band of forty thieves broke into the rich merchant's treasury and took all his gold and valuables. In the morning the Haji woke up to find that his treasury was empty. What a calamity! Unless he recovered his goods the whole edifice of his life and trade would collapse. This would be a disaster not only for him and his family, but for all those he employed; the whole community, in fact, would suffer.

He remembered his *Rammal* and summoned him. 'You must locate the thieves at once, so that we can seize them and recover the content of my treasury,' he commanded.

Hemmat asked for a little time to prepare himself, and went straight home to his wife. 'Well,' he said, 'the catastrophe I have been expecting has arrived; forty thieves broke into my master's treasury last night and took his entire fortune, and he has ordered me to find the miscreants and recover his goods. If I fail, I shall be exposed in front of the whole town, dishonoured, flogged to within an inch of my life and thrown into jail. What will become of us? What can I do now?'

Hemmat was about to burst into tears, but Sediqa remained serene. 'My dear husband! A fine rider you are who falls at the first hurdle! Shame on you for losing faith so quickly. Instead of tearing your hair, go and ask your master for forty days' grace. During that time we will see whether you'll be hanged or hallowed. The Lord is merciful and compassionate,' she soothed him.

The next morning Hemmat repaired to his master's house and begged him for forty days' grace, saying that the situation was complicated, that the stars were in a tricky position and that the knot of this problem required great concentration to unravel. To his surprise Haji Mortaza agreed and Hemmat went home to inform his wife.

'Now what shall I do?' he asked her. 'You know perfectly well that I am totally ignorant of the art of divination, and I can no more read the stars than fly off the roof.'

Sediqa calmed him down again and said, 'Go to the fruit-seller's and buy forty dates. Eat one each evening before your prayer and put the stone into that earthenware jar in the corner, so that we can keep track of your time.'

Hemmat did as he was told and, racked with worry, he ate one date and threw the stone into the jar, saying, 'That was the first of forty.'

Now let me tell you about the forty thieves. They had heard that the rich merchant employed a Master *Rammal* who was so clever and skilful that he could see everything that went on anywhere in the world, even deep in the bowels of the earth and high on the mountain tops, just as if it were there in front of his eyes. They learnt that the *Rammal* had been given forty days to find them and they were scared stiff that wherever they hid he would eventually locate them. They discussed the matter at length among themselves and finally hit on an idea. That evening one of them would creep up to the Chief Astrologer's roof; from there he would spy on him in order to see what he did and how he went about his divination, and come back and report to them.

One of them volunteered to go, and as soon as the sun went down behind the mountains he climbed up on to Hemmat's roof and looked down into his room. At that very moment Hemmat, having eaten his first date, threw the stone into the earthenware jar and said, 'That was the first of forty.' The thief was astounded: surely the Chief *Rammal* was referring to him, the first of forty thieves, and he was frightened out of his wits. He ran back to his partners and gave them the news.

'This *Rammal* is fiendishly clever. No sooner had I got to his roof than I heard him say "That was the first of forty", meaning me of course.'

The robbers couldn't believe their ears. But perhaps that was a coincidence, perhaps the fortune-teller was referring to something else; they had better try again. So the following evening they sent another man up on to Hemmat's roof. Again he reached the place on the roof at the very instant that Hemmat ate a date and threw the stone into the jar, and he heard him say, 'That was the second of forty.'

The thief climbed down from the roof and ran as fast as he could to report to his companions: 'It is true that this *Rammal* is in touch with the Occult World and knows everything; as soon as I reached his roof I heard him call out "That was the second of forty." He obviously meant me, the second of a band of forty robbers.'

The men still could not believe the fortune-teller was warning them, so they sent a third man on the following night and then a fourth, fifth … until every one had heard Hemmat call out his number.

On the last night the thieves gathered and conferred with each other as to the best course of action. They decided that no matter where they hid themselves with their loot, even at the bottom of a well or on top of a mountain, this canny clairvoyant would find them and they would be hanged. It was best to return the stolen goods and ask for mercy.

That night Hemmat hardly slept, for his delay of forty days was up and he did not have the slightest idea where the thieves were or what had happened to the treasure they had stolen. He resigned himself to his fate, got up at the break of day, made his ablutions and said his prayers, and he begged God to perform a miracle and spare his life if only for the sake of his innocent wife and children. He began to set off to Haji Mortaza's house to face the music.

Just as he was about to leave the house, there was a knock on the door. He thought it was his master's servants who had come to fetch him, but instead he found a delegation from the robbers. They came in and swore on the Holy Book that they would show him the hiding place of the treasure if he let them escape unharmed. Hemmat gave them his word of honour. So they led him to a spot in the ruins beyond the city walls where they had hidden the loot in a deep, dry well. Hemmat told them to get away as quickly as they could and not come back to town for a very long time.

You can imagine his joy as he rushed to his master's house with the good news. Once again he had escaped calamity. As soon as the richest merchant in the Bazaar saw him he asked, 'Well, Master *Rammal*, your forty days' grace are over. Have you discovered the thieves' whereabouts?'

Hemmat replied, 'Noble Master, by the Grace of God I have found your treasure hidden in a deep, dry well in the desert beyond the city walls. You need to send your servants with camels and mules to bring it back.'

The merchant went mad with joy. 'But where are the robbers?' he asked.

'Sir, they have escaped beyond our frontiers and it would be costly and dangerous to pursue them. The important thing is that we have found the gold and other valuables intact: not a farthing is missing, you'll see.'

So our clever *Rammal* guided a regiment of servants and camels and mules to the well, and they hauled up the sacks of gold and silver and other valuables.

For his knowledge and sagacity Hemmat was rewarded with money and gems beyond his wildest dreams. He was so elated that his feet hardly touched the ground as he walked home.

'My dear wife,' he said to Sediqa, 'I now have enough money and jewels to live like a soltan, and support seven generations of our descendants. But our situation is still precarious and I must find a way of getting out of fortune-telling and astrology, otherwise sooner or later I'll be found out and lose everything, fame and fortune and honour. You who have always found solutions for our problems thus far, think of what I must do next.'

Sediqa gave the matter some thought and finally told her husband that she had a plan: 'Tomorrow morning when your master goes to the *Hammam*, you must rush in, shove your way through everyone around him, and drag him out of the bath naked. He will think you have gone berserk and he will dismiss you.'

Hemmat thought it was a brilliant idea. The next morning he reached the *Hammam* just as his master had gone into the hot room, and ran towards him. The attendants tried to stop him, but he punched and kicked them out of his way and reached Haji Mortaza, got hold of his legs and dragged him out.

At that very instant the roof of the *Hammam* caved in and tons of masonry came crashing down. Hemmat was astonished and quick as a flash he said, 'You see, Your Honour? I saw in my astrolabe that the roof of the bath was about to collapse, and I rushed in like a lunatic to save you.'

This time Hemmat had not merely saved his master's goods and money but his very life. He was presented with bags of gold and magnificent robes of honour, and his reputation was enhanced tenfold.

In the evening he went home looking despondent. He put his reward down in front of his wife and told her how he had acted on her advice and how it had backfired — instead of being sacked he had been showered with presents.

'What can I do now?' he moaned. 'Can you think of another solution? For it is only a matter of time before my luck turns and I'm unmasked as a fraud.'

Sediqa pondered the matter for a moment and came up with another idea, which this time seemed fool-proof.

'You have told me that on the eve of the Sabbath, in two days' time, your master is giving a grand reception to give thanks for his life being saved. All the notables of the city will be invited. Your master will be sitting on his ceremonial dais exchanging pleasantries with his guests. At that moment you rush in like a raging bull, grab his arm and leg and throw him on the floor. He will be so furious at your impudence that he will think you have taken leave of your senses, and he will sack you on the spot. Then you must come straight home and we'll run away to another province and live quietly there for the rest of our lives.'

'That is the cleverest of all your ideas, my dear wife,' Hemmat retorted, and his anxiety was allayed.

Sure enough a few days later, on the eve of the Sabbath, Haji Mortaza gave a lavish dinner to which he invited all the notables of the town, all the merchants and courtiers and all his important clients. Of course Hemmat was invited as well.

When all the guests had arrived and dinner was about to be served, suddenly there was a commotion, and Hemmat ran in and rushed towards the dais, grabbed his boss's legs and threw him on the floor where he lay spread-eagled. A gasp of horror rose from the assembly as servants hurried to lift the merchant and take away the mad assailant. At that very second a huge scorpion the size of a lizard appeared on the cushion where a minute before the merchant had been resting his back.

Hemmat had no choice but to claim prescience: 'I saw in my astrolabe that Your Excellency was in danger of being stung by a scorpion, so I ran as fast as I could to pull you away from danger.'

This was indeed a miracle; once again the Chief *Rammal* had saved his master's life. This time Hemmat was given two bags of gold, plus some precious stones, but instead of being happy he went home in despair, telling his wife what had happened.

'Don't be despondent,' Sediqa consoled him. 'My good husband, I have no more ideas. Put the matter in God's hands and see what happens, for He is merciful and compassionate.'

Hemmat resigned himself to his fate and tried not to fret. One day his master decided to go hunting, and he asked his Chief Astrologer if the stars were favourable. Hemmat consulted his *Rammal* boards and astrolabe and assured him that they were. His master insisted that he accompany him, for he had become his most trusted and favoured servant.

As the Haji was riding at the head of the expedition a grasshopper alighted on his saddle in front of him. He caught it and hid it in his hand, then he called his *Rammal* forward and said to him jokingly, 'Now guess what I have got in my hand.'

Hemmat nearly fell off his horse with panic. 'This time I've had it,' he thought to himself. 'What I have been dreading all along has finally arrived and there is no escape.' He remembered the old saying, that one can get away with a lie once or twice but in the end one will be caught: 'The grasshopper hopped once, the grasshopper hopped twice, and now the grasshopper is caught in the palm of a hand,' he said to himself.

He decided to repeat this old proverb aloud and beg for mercy. 'The grasshopper hopped once, the grasshopper hopped twice, and now the grasshopper is caught in the palm of a hand,' he recited. The richest merchant in the Bazaar was speechless at the wisdom and knowledge of his Chief *Rammal.* He laughed and opened his hand and let the grasshopper fly away.

That evening Hemmat went home and told Sediqa the story. She said that since God evidently wished him to carry on being a

Rammal, he should resign himself to His Will, instead of trying to fight it.

Not long after this Haji Mortaza died, leaving Hemmat a large legacy. So he was able to retire and live happily ever after with his beloved Sediqa and their children.

The Story of Bijan and Manijeh

There was one and there was none/Except for God there was no one.

Long, long ago, in the reign of King Kay Khosro, there was a young warrior in Persia called Bijan. He was the grandson of Rustam, the greatest hero the world has ever known, the son of Rustam's beautiful daughter Banou Goshasp. Bijan was so handsome and brave that every woman who saw him immediately fell in love with him. He could have married any of the accomplished young ladies of the Court, even the King's own daughter, but he was not interested. He was too full of dreams of glory and conquest to think of love and marriage; his only desire was for victory in battle, so he could prove himself worthy of his illustrious grandfather, Rustam.

When Bijan was growing up, Persia was often at war with Touran, a kingdom in the East whose king, Afrasiab, was also a famous warrior. He was belligerent, and he periodically attacked Persia and invaded the Eastern provinces, only to be pushed back, defeated by the powerful Persian army and its famous heroes, of whom the most celebrated was the invincible Rustam. They said Rustam's back had never touched the ground, and that even in old age he could lift an enemy in full armour and whirl him above his head like a puppet, before putting him down and sitting on his chest in triumph. He had even fought the *divs* in Mazandaran and annihilated them, ridding the country of their tyranny.

Bijan was impatient to take part in a battle and he chafed like a young colt at the harness. When he finally reached maturity at the age of sixteen, it happened that Afrasiab once again attacked Persia. There was no holding Bijan back — he hurled himself into battle and immediately distinguished himself. He proved himself as strong, agile and intrepid as his grandfather, and all the older warriors who had fought alongside Rustam immediately recognized his mettle. He spread fear through enemy ranks and dispatched many of their best warriors. In those days they didn't have all the machines of today, guns and aeroplanes and tanks; it was just men in armour fighting with swords and maces and chains and slings, but what determined the final outcome was often a one-to-one wrestling match between two individual warriors.

Anyway, Bijan showed exceptional ability in every way, but his hour of triumph was when he recovered the Persian flag, the famous Kaviani Banner. How had it disappeared? How could such a thing have happened? The flag represented the very spirit of Persia, the triumph of Good over Evil as a result of human effort. How could it have fallen into enemy hands?

Well, what had happened was that, faced with the enemy's tremendous onslaught, Fariborz, the commander of the Persian army, had suddenly panicked and fled from the field, taking the flag with him. As a result the Persian army, bereft of its emblem and guiding spirit, had begun to lose heart. Defeat was looming, and the only salvation was to find the flag and bring it back.

Without a moment's hesitation, Bijan set off in pursuit of the fugitive. He rode with the speed of a dart and caught up with Fariborz, wrested the flag from his hand and brought it back. Then, holding it aloft and galloping through the ranks, he restored the morale of the army. The Persians, exalted by the recovery of their standard, fought like lions and won the battle. Afrasiab and his army were routed and fled.

But none of these exploits were unusual, and Bijan would be only one famous warrior among many were it not for his greatest conquest: the heart of Manijeh, Afrasiab's daughter, famous for her beauty and accomplishments. It is their love story that has kept Bijan and Manijeh alive in the hearts and minds of all lovers to this day and forever more. For it is the undying light of Love that illumines the universe, while kingdoms rise and fall, soltans triumph and die, and in the end all mortal bodies are turned to dust.

One day King Kay Khosro was celebrating his latest victory over his old enemy Afrasiab. The throne-room was decorated with triumphal colours and the King, clad in splendid robes and wearing his crown, sat on the throne surrounded by his generals and war heroes. Wine flowed like liquid rubies, scrumptious dishes followed one after another, while musicians played and angel-faced girls with ivory skin and black flowing hair, fragrant with the attar of musk, attended to the guests.

Suddenly a guard rushed in and, bowing deeply before the King, announced that a delegation had come with an urgent petition from the North, from near the frontier with Touran. He informed the King that the men were distraught and exhausted after their long journey, and although they did not wish to disturb His Majesty's revels, they begged immediate audience.

The King ordered that they be led in to his presence, and they informed him that a great calamity had befallen them: their land was devastated by an invasion of wild boars, big, ferocious beasts with huge tusks which were destroying their woods and fields and killing their livestock. They had tried everything, but such was the animals' numbers and strength that nothing could stop them: they stampeded over hedges and with one thrust of a tusk killed any man who dared to tackle them. The local pastures and fields were reduced to wilderness, their animals decimated and their woodlands ravaged. They had reached the end of their tether and only the King, protector of the defenceless and dispenser of justice, could rescue them.

What could the King do? He looked round the hall at his warriors and generals, who were flushed with the pride of victory and the spirit of wine, and asked who among them wished to undertake the mission of ridding the land of this latest scourge. By way of encouragement he offered ten steeds of the highest pedigree, apparelled with gold and brocade, and a large tray of gems and jewellery to whoever volunteered.

There was a moment of silence when everyone lowered his gaze and held his breath, wondering who would dare to come forward. Nobody moved. Certainly the reward was huge, but so was the danger. They had just escaped death in battle and they did not wish to tempt Fate.

Then, to everyone's astonishment Bijan, the youngest of them all, rose and put himself at the King's disposal. His father, Giv, tried to dissuade him, warning him of the enormous odds against the enterprise, saying that a single large boar was enough to kill half a dozen men, while as for hundreds of wild boars ... But Bijan was determined. 'Do not underestimate me, dear Father,' he said. 'I may be young in years but my judgement is sound, and I'm confident I shall succeed.'

The King was delighted and he turned to Gorgin, another young warrior, saying, 'Go with him, for you know the area well, and you can be his guide and companion.' And without any more ado the two young men left the assembly and set off on their mission.

Bijan and Gorgin rode and rode, day and night, until they reached the forest of the wild boars and saw the havoc they had wrought through the land. Bijan's heart was filled with pity and his blood boiled with anger. Tired and hungry after their long journey, the two young men needed a meal and some rest before beginning their task. They caught a pig with their lasso, killed it, made a fire and roasted the pig on a spit. They ate the succulent meat, drank wine and lay down in the shade of a tree, all the while discussing the best way of tackling the animals.

'I will shower my arrows at them while you go around with your mace and dagger, kill as many as you can and finish off the wounded to prevent any further attacks, and that way we can get them all,' Bijan suggested.

Gorgin was terrified. He had no wish to enter this dangerous battle fray and he protested. 'Since it was you who volunteered for this task,' he said, 'and it was you who received the horses and jewels from the King, it should be you, not me, who fights these boars.' He added, 'My duty was to be your guide and companion, and I have fulfilled it.'

Bijan was disappointed at his friend's reaction. Nevertheless, undaunted, when the next morning they entered the forest, he roared like a lion and attacked the animals alone. Arrows flashed and hissed in all directions like lightning, hitting and wounding the pigs as they shrieked and grunted and stampeded away. Bijan pursued them. Stabbing with dagger and hurling his mace and lasso in every direction, he fought the beasts as if he had ten arms and hands. Some of the larger pigs fought back ferociously, tearing up trees with their tusks and raising clouds of dust, while branches and leaves fell like rain and the forest became as dark as a moonless night. In the mayhem a huge black boar with tusks as large as an elephant's hurled himself at Bijan and tore his coat of mail, but Bijan plunged his dagger into its throat and the pig fell to the ground, mortally wounded. He then turned to the others, killing them left, right and centre, until none was left and the forest was strewn with their corpses.

Watching the scene from a safe distance, Gorgin was lost in admiration for Bijan's intrepid courage, his speed and his skill. He felt ashamed of his own cowardice and the Evil of Envy entered his soul. He did not show his feelings; instead, he congratulated his friend on his success and showered him with compliments, saying he had taken part in many battles and hunts and seen many re-nowned hunters and warriors, but never in all his life had he witnessed such prowess as Bijan had just demonstrated. Bijan was glad of his friend's compliments and forgave him his weakness, not knowing that Gorgin was full of Envy and that he was planning to harm him, for the pure in heart do not suspect base motives in others.

When the dust of the battle had settled, the villagers rushed to the scene, expressing their gratitude to Bijan. They blessed him and rejoiced, and they prepared a feast to celebrate his victory. They ate and drank, and Bijan rested a while to recover his strength before starting the return journey.

Meanwhile Gorgin was plotting a scheme. He told Bijan that he knew the region well and that not far away, at the frontier of Touran, there was a beautiful glade, with meadows and gardens that were always full of flowers and birdsong. Every year, in this very season, Afrasiab's renowned daughter Manijeh and her com-panions escaped from the constraints of the Court and spent a few days enjoying themselves there, bathing in the springs and pools and singing, dancing and playing music like *houris* in Paradise. He suggested that as a reward for Bijan's triumph, they made a detour to this glade, where he could watch the beautiful Tourani girls at their revels.

Bijan let himself be tempted and they set off at once. They galloped for two days, stopping only to eat and sleep, and finally they reached the crest of a hill at the frontier of Touran. Before them spread a sparkling green valley, carpeted with velvety grass and wild flowers. The air was fragrant with the scent of musk, full of the murmur of streams and the song of nightingales; water as refreshing as nectar gushed from the springs. Tents had been pitched just outside a wood and a bevy of young beauties in their fineries were fluttering about like butterflies in a meadow. Among them the tall, regal Manijeh shone like the moon in a starry sky.

Bijan was enchanted. He longed to get closer and have a better look. Instead of warning him of the danger of entering enemy territory, Gorgin encouraged him. 'Go!' he said. 'Go and enjoy yourself, you have deserved it.' But first Bijan had to prepare himself. He bathed in the stream and dressed in fine clothes, put on his jewel-encrusted hero's hat and rode down towards the wood near the encampment. He tied his horse to a cypress and sat in the shade of a willow tree where he had a good view of the party.

Presently Manijeh came out of her tent and saw him. She was struck by his beauty, and wondered who he was and how he had come to be there. Was he a human being or an angel? For he was unlike any man she had ever seen. His robes and his hat indicated a prince or a hero. She sent her nurse to find out who the handsome stranger was, where he came from, whether he was human or from the race of *paris*, and to invite him to their camp.

The Nurse duly delivered the message. 'I'm not an angel nor am I from the race of *paris*. I am from Persia, the land of free men,' he said. Accepting Manijeh's gracious invitation, he followed the Nurse to her tent.

Manijeh came forward and greeted him with open arms. 'I am Manijeh, daughter of Afrasiab,' she said. 'Who are you? I have come to this glade year after year and never have I seen your equal.'

Bijan introduced himself and Manijeh undid his warrior's belt and sword, took him by the hand and led him in. He sat beside her and told her his story, how he had been sent by King Kay Khosro to free the land from a plague of wild boars, how he had fought them single-handedly until he had slain them all, and how he had made a detour before going back home.

Manijeh ordered a grand feast in his honour. It lasted three days and three nights, with music and dancing, with wine flowing and time flying, as if there were no tomorrow.

But all such festivities, alas, come to an end. It was time for Bijan to go back to Persia and for Manijeh to return to the city. But she had fallen ocean-deep in love with Bijan and could not bear to part from him. She called in a magus and asked him to prepare a strong sleeping potion, which she secretly poured into Bijan's cup. As soon as he drank it, he fell into a deep sleep and Manijeh wrapped him in a silken sheet and took him to her Palace. She sat beside him, contemplating his innocent face, her heart brimming with love, until he woke up.

When Bijan noticed his surroundings he realized what had happened, and he began to curse Gorgin. He understood that Gorgin had led him into this trap, that far from being his guide and companion, he had led him astray, and that he himself would never return home alive.

Manijeh soothed him, telling him to take life as it came, saying he had nothing to worry about, and that if her father Afrasiab discovered them, she would shield him with her own body. 'Let us enjoy ourselves and be happy,' she urged him and she did all she could to make their life a permanent feast.

One day, when Bijan was walking in the garden, a guard saw him and denounced him to Afrasiab, telling the King that his daughter had taken a Persian as consort and was living with him in her Palace. Afrasiab was thunder-struck. He could not believe that his dutiful, loving daughter could be so impious, and he sent his Vizir to verify the story.

Accompanied by a hundred armed guardsmen the Vizir arrived at Manijeh's Palace and found it full of light and music and laughter, as if some great celebration were taking place. He followed the sound to the banqueting-room, and there, sitting beside Manijeh on a dais and surrounded by a bevy of young girls and beautiful *saqis* and dancers, was a splendid youth — Bijan. The Vizir ordered his soldiers to seize him and, ignoring Manijeh's entreaties, he took the captive to Afrasiab.

Afrasiab was so furious that he wanted to kill the young man there and then, but Bijan begged him to listen to his story. He told him everything — the battle against the wild boars, the detour to the birdsong glade, the encounter with Manijeh. He added that Manijeh was innocent, that her heart was pure, and that she had done nothing blameworthy; only he, Bijan, was to blame.

Afrasiab heard him out, but his fury was unabated, and he condemned Bijan to death by hanging. In the meantime, while the gallows were being prepared, he threw him into a dungeon. Left alone in his dark cell, Bijan began to lament his youth, and the sorrow and shame he was bringing to his father Giv and his grandfather Rustam. He cursed Gorgin for his betrayal, and he prayed to God to save his life and his honour.

It seems that his prayers were heard, for as the gallows were being erected in the Public Square and the crowd was gathering for Bijan's execution, one of Afrasiab's most famous old warriors, Piran, happened to pass by.

He asked who it was they were hanging, and he was told about Bijan and his crime. Piran had witnessed Bijan's prowess in the battlefield and knew who he was, and he asked for a stay of execution. 'Stop!' he said to the executioner. 'Wait until I come back with

confirmation of this order from the King.' The executioner agreed
— such was the respect and affection the old warrior enjoyed.

Without a second's delay, Piran hurried to Afrasiab's Palace
and, waving aside the usual protocol, rushed to the King and told
him he was about to commit an irreparable folly.

'Do you know who this young man is?' he said to Afrasiab. 'He
is the son of Banou Goshasp and Giv, and the grandson of the great
Rustam. If you hang him, the Persians will wreak such revenge
upon us that nothing will remain of our army and our country. If
you must punish him, keep him in prison.'

Reluctantly Afrasiab accepted Piran's advice. He ordered that
Bijan be tied from head to foot in heavy iron chains and thrown
into a deep, dry well in the wilderness outside the city, that the
well be covered with a large stone, and that he be left there until
the end of his life.

When Manijeh heard of Bijan's fate, she wept and wept and
sank into despair. Meanwhile Afrasiab sent his Vizir to strip his
wretched daughter of her crown and all her possessions, and throw
her out of the city.

The Vizir duly obeyed the King's orders and Manijeh found
herself alone and bereft in the desert, beside the well where Bijan
was imprisoned. She could not move the heavy stone, but she
found a chink on the side of the well which she managed to enlarge
enough to communicate with her beloved. They talked and com-
miserated with and consoled each other, and Manijeh set about to
beg for food and to secure some nourishment to keep her beloved
alive while they waited for Providence to rescue them.

Now let us go back to Persia. Gorgin waited for a whole week
for Bijan to come back from his escapade with Manijeh, growing
ever more anxious and contrite. Eventually he realized that his
scheme had worked and that Bijan would never come out of Touran alive. 'Oh God! What have I done?' he moaned, mortified by

his own treachery and bitterly regretting it. His heart and mind torn by remorse, he recovered Bijan's horse from the meadow where he had been abandoned, rode back to the capital and went straight to Bijan's house to report his loss to his father Giv.

As soon as Giv saw Gorgin arrive and saw Bijan's horse with no rider, his heart sank. He uttered a cry of anguish to pierce a stone and began to lament, saying, 'God has given me only one son whom I love more than my own life, the noblest and bravest young warrior in the world, worthy seed of the great Rustam. What has happened to him? Tell me the truth.'

Gorgin told him his version of their journey to the forest near the frontier of Touran, how they had fought like lions with the teeming crowd of wild boars until they had slain them all and rid the land of their presence. Then passing through a green valley on their return journey, they had suddenly seen a wild ass, a magnificent specimen, with the grace of a peacock and the speed of a leopard. 'Bijan wanted to capture it at all costs,' Gorgin went on with the story. 'He threw his lasso to capture it, but the animal bolted, pulling Bijan with him. A cloud of dust rose up and they disappeared from my view. I galloped after them and searched everywhere, all through the valley and the wilderness beyond, but I found no trace of either the hunter or his prey until I came across this horse, and after waiting several days in vain, I came back.'

Gorgin was pale and distraught, his heart full of remorse and fear, while the grief-stricken Giv was so angry with him for failing to protect his son that he wanted to kill him there and then, but he restrained himself. Instead he took him to King Kay Khosro to let him decide his fate.

When the King heard the story, his heart was touched by Giv's sorrow and he felt suspicious of Gorgin. He soothed the stricken father by saying that his son was surely alive, that he must have strayed in his pursuit of the wild ass and entered Touran, where he was doubtless being held as hostage. He promised to gather the biggest army ever seen and wage war against the Touranians and liberate Bijan. Giv was somewhat reassured and thanked the King for his compassion.

Now King Kay Khosro had a cup called *Jam-e Gitty-Nama* — the World-Reflecting Cup — so called because when he looked into it he could see the whole world, East and West, from China to Byzantium. He asked for it to be brought to him and he looked into it to find out Bijan's whereabouts. Having scanned the whole world he saw Touran, and there in a deep, dark well, wrapped in chains, was Bijan.

He told Giv to rejoice: his son was alive, though a captive of Afrasiab. Giv was relieved and he thanked God for His mercy. But how were they to rescue Bijan? He could not last long as he was and the odds against the success of a raid were enormous. After much deliberation they came to the conclusion that no one was up to this task except the great Rustam himself. He alone would be able to overcome any difficulty and remove any obstacle, as he had done many times before. So the King wrote a letter to Rustam in which he explained Bijan's predicament and asked for his help, and he asked Giv to deliver it. Meanwhile Gorgin was chained and thrown into a dark dungeon, where he was gnawed by shame and remorse.

Now Rustam, having won many battles against Afrasiab and defeated the *divs* in Mazandaran, had retired to his home in Sistan to spend a peaceful old age in a region hundreds of leagues away from the Court. Giv rode non-stop until he reached Sistan and went straight to Rustam's Palace to deliver the King's letter.

Rustam welcomed his son-in-law with warmth and due ceremony, but when he read the King's letter his brow darkened and his eyes clouded. Bijan's predicament was unusual and he needed to think. After a while he said to Giv that with the Grace of God he had defeated all the enemies of Persia, and he hoped to be successful in this mission as well.

'Meanwhile you are exhausted by your journey,' he said to Giv. 'You must rest a while and regain your strength while we prepare for the expedition.'

He gave a great feast in his guest's honour, one that lasted three days, with food and wine and music. By the fourth day everything was ready and they set out on their journey at full speed.

Rustam had a horse called Rakhsh, who rode with the speed of lightning, like the winged mount of the Archangel Gabriel. He had served Rustam in all his battles and would submit to no other master; anyone else who attempted to ride him, even the most skilful horseman, was thrown off ignominiously. Rustam ordered Rakhsh to be saddled and, accompanied by Giv and one hundred of his best warriors, he set off for the capital.

They rode day and night until they arrived at the royal Court. They were at once received by the King with the warmest greetings. Everyone was delighted to see the great hero again and a sumptuous banquet was given in his honour.

When Gorgin heard that Rustam was coming to see the King, he guessed that the purpose of his visit was to plan Bijan's rescue. For the first time since his disgrace he saw a glimmer of hope. He sent a message to Rustam expressing bitter regret for his cowardice and disloyalty, saying that he was willing to lay down his life to redeem himself, and he begged Rustam to plead with the King on his behalf.

Rustam replied that when a man allows base passions to overcome his reason, he forfeits his honour and sovereignty. Even if the King forgave Gorgin, Giv would not, not until his son was released. Nonetheless, with the magnanimity of a true hero, he asked Kay Khosro to forgive Gorgin. The King was adamant: as long as Bijan remained in chains, so too would Gorgin. But Rustam pleaded on his behalf, saying that Gorgin knew the terrain and would be useful on the expedition. In the end he persuaded the King to set him free.

After much thought and discussion, Rustam said to the King that war was not the best option: since Afrasiab was known to harbour grudges he might kill Bijan in revenge. Cunning would work better and he had worked out a plan: he would disguise himself as an old merchant, and disguise his soldiers as his companions and servants, and take a caravan of merchandise to Touran. Not until he had found and released Bijan would he surprise Afrasiab with a night attack and destroy his army.

The King approved Rustam's plan and gave him permission to choose anything he wanted from his treasury to present as merchandise. Ten camels were loaded with gold, another hundred with all kinds of desirable goods — gems and jewels, fine cloths and garments, spices and attars — and the caravan set off to the sound of bugles and bells.

After many days they reached the city of Khatan in Touran, whose governor was Piran, the old and wise Tourani hero who had persuaded Afrasiab to spare Bijan's life. In those days there were no photographs and many years had passed since the two men had met on the battlefield, weighed down with armour. They had both aged since then and Piran did not recognize his famous adversary. But Rustam's noble countenance and handsome figure indicated his important position. After the usual greetings, he offered Rustam hospitality at his own castle, but Rustam preferred to be independent and he chose separate quarters. Soon the news spread that a Persian merchant had arrived in the city, bringing magnificent goods, and people rushed to buy from him.

Now let us go back to Manijeh and Bijan. Manijeh begged for food and she dropped it down the well to Bijan to keep him alive. As soon as she heard that a caravan had arrived from Persia her heart filled with hope. Barefoot and dressed in rags, she ran to Rustam's camp and pushing away servants and guards rushed straight to his quarters.

'I am Manijeh, daughter of Afrasiab,' she introduced herself. 'I was once a princess who vied with the sun in glory, but for the love of a Persian youth, Bijan, I lost my crown and my power, and now you see me in rags, my once radiant face yellow and awash with tears. But more unfortunate than me is Bijan, who is at the bottom of a deep, dark well, tied up in heavy chains. You must know his father Giv and grandfather Rustam at the Court of King Kay Khosro. Go and tell them Bijan's story, and ask them to come and save him.'

Rustam at first denied any knowledge of Giv or Rustam, saying that he was only a merchant going about his business and that he did not know the King or his officers, but seeing Manijeh's tears of despair and touched by her constancy and courage, he relented. He asked for some food to be brought in, and taking a roast chicken, he secretly inserted his ring inside it. He then wrapped the chicken in a flat bread which he gave to Manijeh to take to her beloved, promising her to do what he could.

Manijeh went to the well, dropped down the bird and told Bijan about the caravan of Persian merchants. As the starving prisoner unwrapped the bread and uncovered the bird, he saw Rustam's ring. He cried with joy — this ring was the key to his salvation. He confided in Manijeh that the merchant she had seen was none other than the great Rustam himself, that the purpose of his expedition must be Bijan's rescue and nothing else. 'Go and tell him that I have recognized his ring and that I know my ordeals will soon be over.'

He then turned his gaze to Heaven and thanked the Creator for his mercy, while Manijeh returned to Rustam with Bijan's message. Rustam asked Manijeh to gather some wood and light a fire at night by Bijan's well to guide them. Manijeh agreed.

At dusk she gathered some brambles and thorns and stacked them by the well in a huge pile. When darkness deepened and the sky turned pitch black, she lit the fire and gave Rustam the signal.

Rustam put on his armour and, with a handful of his best men, he went to the well. The men tried to move the stone but they found it impossible, so the invincible hero dismounted. With one heave of his shoulders he shifted the stone. A shaft of light penetrated the dark well and Bijan uttered a cry of relief, calling out the hero's name.

Rustam addressed him with words of comfort and added, 'I have one request from you before I lift you up, and that is to forgive Gorgin.'

It was like a knife in Bijan's heart. 'Gorgin is responsible for my plight,' he said. 'He led me to a trap and caused all my misery. How can I forgive him?'

But Rustam insisted, saying that it was the privilege of heroes to be magnanimous and forgive their enemies. Anyway, Gorgin had already paid for his error and was even ready to swap places with him.

Finally Bijan relented and agreed to forgive his friend. Rustam then threw his rope down and pulled the prisoner up. Oh what a pitiful sight! The handsome young man, once as erect as a cypress tree and as radiant as the sun, was now an emaciated old caveman, covered with cuts and sores, his hair and nails as long as an animal's, his sallow skin coated with blood and mud, his eyes lustreless and half-blind. Rustam took him into his arms, comforted him and carried him back to his encampment. Bijan was washed, his wounds were dressed and covered with balm, and he put on fine clothes. Manijeh, too, was attended to, and her beauty shone once again.

Then Rustam confronted Afrasiab in his Palace and poured scorn on him for what he had done to Bijan. Afrasiab called out his army and before dawn battle was joined between the two adversaries. Afrasiab lost the contest and Rustam returned home in triumph.

King Kay Khosro gave him a hero's welcome — the whole city was illuminated with lights and fireworks and the population rejoiced. Rustam put on his hero's helmet and girded himself with his royal belt and attended the feast at the Court.

King Kay Khosro called Bijan forward and asked him to tell his story. They all listened with amazement at his adventures and gave thanks to God, without whose Grace all human effort is futile. And Bijan and Manijeh lived together happily ever after.

Our story is told and you must rest
Though the crow has not yet reached its nest.

Notes

Foreword

[1] Imam Ali is the son-in-law of the Prophet, also the first Imam of the Duodecimal Shiites, and the patron saint of Sufis and mystics of all hues.

[2] The first verse of the Quran: 'In the name of God, the Infinitely Merciful, the All Compassionate.'

[3] Matthew Arnold's poem 'Sohrab and Rustum' gives a flavour of the passionate eloquence of Firdowsi's story in English.

[4] Bruno Bettelheim, *The Uses of Enchantment*.

[5] Sigmund Freud, *Collected Works*, vol 12: *The Occurrence in Dreams of Material from Fairy Tales*.

[6] Carl Jung, *Collected Works*, vol 9: *Archetypes and the Collective Unconscious — The Phenomenology of the Spirit in the Fairy Tales*.

[7] For a complete collection of stories from the *Shahnameh* see Dick Davies's magnificent three-volume prose translation: Mage Publishers/I.B. Tauris.

The Padishah and His Three Daughters

[1] *Kowthar* is the stream in Paradise, mentioned in the Quran.

[2] *Gohar-Shab-Cheraq* is a huge diamond, like the *Kuh-e-Nur*.

The Thief and the Cunning Bride

1 Muslim Lent, month of fasting.

2 See note 1 to 'The Padishah and His Three Daughters', above.

The Talking Skull

1 A pilau made with rice, red barberries, pistachios, almond slivers and shredded orange peel. The different colours make it look like a piece of jewellery.

The Magic Saucepan and the Piece of Lamb's Tail

1 The breed of Persian lamb with a round tail of pure fat, much appreciated for its taste, used in soups and stews.

2 The formula is used as a mark of woe and loss.

The Secret of Laughter

1 The construction was called 'wind-catcher' — *bad-gir* — and the room below had a fountain in the middle, around which the family sat in summer to keep cool while air circulated.

The King and the Prophet Khizr

1 A boat-shaped bowl which can serve as a container, made of silver or copper, with a chain handle.

2 The poem is by the thirteenth-century poet Saadi.

The Cruel Mother-in-Law

1 A large nap spread on the floor on which plates and food are arranged. Eating at a table is a Western import.

The Man Whose Luck Had Gone to Sleep

1 The equivalent of 'My luck has turned'.

2 The Persian expression *Kaleh-Khoshk* is literally 'dry-brained'. The brain being soft and moist, dryness stands for senility.

I Know That Already

1 A substantial soup eaten with bread.
2 Stew made with lamb or poultry, walnuts and pomegranate juice.
3 In Persian *Fout-e-kasehgar*. It refers to when a glass-maker blows on the molten glass to cool it.

The Good Vizir and His Pride

1 Soltan Mahmoud of Ghazneh, the founder of the Ghaznavy dynasty in the twelfth century, was from Central Asia and Turkish speaking, hence the title Soltan (Sultan), which is Turkish for King. Many legends are attributed to him and this is one of them.
2 Shepherd's cloak made of felt.
3 Exchange of pleasantries to mark respect and affection.
4 The equivalent of his luck turning.

The Good Young Man and the Heavenly Woman

1 A *pari* is both a fairy and an angel.

The Thorn-Seller and the Bird of Paradise

1 Mashti is short for Mashhadi, a title given to those who have made the pilgrimage to Meshed, where Imam Reza, the Eighth Imam of the Duo-decimal Shiites, is buried.

Soltan Mahmoud and the Band of Robbers

1 See note 1 to 'The Good Vizir and His Pride', above.
2 Leyly and Majnoun are legendary star-crossed lovers, much written about by poets.

List of Persian Words

Ab-gousht	substantial lamb soup eaten with bread
âbed	ascetic
adab	formal courtesy
Alam-e-Gheib	the Occult or Invisible World
andaroun	the women's quarters of a large house
Aql	Reason
Ash	thick soup made with rice, herbs and pulses
bad-gir	wind-catcher
barakat	divine blessing
bazaarcheh	little bazaar
birouni	the men's quarters of a large house
caravanserai	inn for caravans
chai-khaneh	tea house
dallak	bath attendant who massages, scrubs and washes the clients in the *Hammam*
dirham	shilling
div	giant demons
donbeh	lamb tail-fat
Elm-e-Gheib	knowledge of the Occult World

eyvan	domed veranda
Farangi	'Frank' or French, and by extension all Europeans
Farangistan	Europe
fessenjan	stew made with lamb or poultry, walnuts and pomegranate juice.
Fout-e-kasehgar	literally 'breath of the glass-blower'; refers to when a glass-maker blows on the molten glass to cool it
Gohar-Shab-Cheraq	a huge diamond
haji	one who has accomplished the pilgrimage to Mecca
Hajj	the pilgrimage to Mecca, a compulsory religious duty for the wealthy
halva	sweetmeat made with flour, butter, sugar and saffron
Hammam	public baths
houri	nymph
kapanak	shepherd's cloak made of felt
kashkoul	dervish's bowl
khar-kan	thorn-seller
Kowthar	stream in Paradise, mentioned in the Quran
madrasah	medieval college
maktab	primary school
mounis	lady-in-waiting
naqqal	professional story-teller
nargileh	waterpipe, hubble-bubble
noql	sweetmeat made with slivers of almond covered with sugar
pari	fairy and angel
qaran	shilling
Qazi	religious judge
Qismat	Fate, lot
Ramadan	Muslim Lent, a month of fasting
Rammal	fortune-teller and astrologer

saqi	cup-bearer
shireh	a kind of molasses
sofreh	nap
taarof	exchange of courtesies to mark respect and affection
tanour	clay oven for baking bread
vird	magic formula
zahr-e-halal	deadly poison
zur-khaneh	traditional gymnasium